NOODLE!

MIMI AYE

100 AMAZING
AUTHENTIC RECIPES

NOODLE!

100 AMAZING AUTHENTIC RECIPES

First published in Great Britain in 2014 by Absolute Press, an imprint of Bloomsbury Publishing Plc

Absolute Press
Scarborough House
29 James Street West
Bath BA1 2BT
Phone 44 (0) 1225 316013
Fax 44 (0) 1225 445836
E-mail office@absolutepress.co.uk
Website www.absolutepress.co.uk

Publisher Jon Croft
Commissioning Editor Meg Avent
Art Direction and Design Matt Inwood
Project Editor Alice Gibbs
Editor Norma MacMillan
Photography Mike Cooper
Food Styling Genevieve Taylor

ISBN: 9781472905673

Printed and bound in China by C&C Printing.

Bloomsbury Publishing Plc
50 Bedford Square
London WC1B 3DP
www.bloomsbury.com

Bloomsbury is a trademark of Bloomsbury Publishing Plc

A note about the text

This book was set using ITC Century and Serifa. The first Century typeface was cut in 1894. In 1975, an updated family of Century typefaces was designed by Tony Stan for ITC. The Serifa font was designed by Adrian Frutiger in 1978.

Thanks

Thank you first and foremost to my husband Simon, my parents U Zaw Min and Daw Khin Hnin Wai, and my in-laws Sheila and Martin for all their love and support.

Thank you to my agent Juliet Pickering at Blake Friedmann and Jon, Matt and Alice at Absolute Press for believing in me, and thank you to Gen and Mike for the stunning photos.

Thanks to Mat Follas for getting me into this food lark in the first place, to Graham Holliday for getting me into blogging, and to Marina O'Loughlin and Craig Brown for the (comic) inspiration.

Lastly, thanks to my old school teachers Colin Simpson, Charles Dormer and Stan Wolfson – I learnt more about the written word from them than anyone else.

This book is for my beloved baby daughter Thida, who tried her very best to stop me writing it. Let's hope I'm less sleep-deprived for the next one, eh?

About MiMi Aye

An obsession with food, especially Burmese cuisine, led to MiMi starting www.meemalee.com where she shares her culinary thoughts, recipes and reviews. Due to her eloquent and often wry turn of phrase, her blog is popular worldwide, although particularly in the Netherlands for reasons she has never been able to fathom.

Recommended by *Lonely Planet* and *Time Out*, MiMi has appeared on BBC Radio 4's *Food Programme*, in the *Guardian*, the *Telegraph* and *Metro*. Her recipes featured on Channel 4 Food to accompany the TV show *Gordon Ramsay's Great Escapes*.

She lives in Kent with her husband, her daughter, and a collection of gashapon.

Opposite:
Tempura Crumb Udon (Tanuki Udon), page 55

If you're looking for an in-depth history of noodles, I suggest you look elsewhere.

I am not a noodle expert or anthropologist, and when I look at the shelves of noodles on offer in the Chinese supermarket, I'm as giddied by the choice as anyone else. However, if you're looking for someone to tell you how to cook oodles of wondrous noodles and provide the odd bit of noodle-based trivia, I'm definitely your woman.

I am a noodle enthusiast – an avid eater and an equally eager cook, which you'll see from the food blog I write at meemalee.com. My parents are from Burma (aka Myanmar), where noodles are a way of life – the national dish is *Mohinga*, a bowl of fish chowder with slippery rice noodles, fresh feathery coriander, crunchy white cabbage and crispy pea fritters.

The Burmese word for noodles is *khao swè*, which literally means 'fold / pull'*, and is a reference to how they were traditionally made – by folding and pulling dough repeatedly until strands of noodles were formed. And so, there are recipes here that take you back to tradition, and teach you how to make your own noodles from scratch. There are also recipes here that use the humble instant noodle – there is no such thing as a bad noodle in my book (pun intended). And if you're missing an old favourite, I hope you'll discover a new noodle love.

Most of the hundred dishes come from Asia, and China is generally considered the birthplace of the noodle – in fact, a 4000-year-old bowl of millet-based noodles was unearthed in Lajia in China in 2002. As noodle dishes spread from China, they morphed and were adapted over time to use unique local flavours and ingredients. So you will see that some of these recipes are distant cousins, although they deserve to be documented separately as wonderful dishes in their own right.

A few of the recipes may look a little long and complicated, but please believe me when I say they're worth the wait (and effort). Others, though, are ready in minutes and use only a handful of ingredients, but are no less delicious because of this.

As a fairly neutral ingredient, noodles can take on all sorts of flavours or act as a foil to dishes that are spicy or soothing, rich or light. They can also vary in texture, from silky smooth to satisfyingly crunchy – see my recipe for Bombay Mix, for example.

The main thing I want you to take away from this book is how wonderfully versatile noodles can be – whether you're planning a quick desk lunch, an easy weeknight meal, a weekend treat, a lavish feast or even a picnic, you'll find the perfect noodle dish for you.

MiMi Aye
London, January 2014

*Unfortunately for generations of Burmese children, khao swè also means 'knock / yank'. Older siblings will ask them, 'Khao swè sar-ma-lar? [Do you want to eat noodles?]' and when the unsuspecting innocents say yes, they are greeted by a sharp rap on the head and a yank of their hair (I have suffered in this way).

Opposite:
Saucy Chicken and Peanut Noodles (Gaw-yay Khao Swè), page 116

NOODLES

This book uses the word 'noodle' in its British English sense, so we're talking long, thin strips of dough. The dough is usually made from cereals or pulses, but there are also recipes using noodles made from vegetables such as sweet potato and something called devil's tongue (a type of yam). Here's a description of the noodles used in this book.

Wheat Noodles

• *ban mian* or *pan mee* – a hand-torn noodle from China and Malaysia; home-made by tearing off rough, flat pieces of dough and boiling immediately.

• *chūkamen* – a thin, pale yellow Japanese noodle; served hot in ramen and yakisoba, and cold in *Hiyashi Chūka*. Found fresh, dried or frozen in packets in Japanese supermarkets, and fresh or dried in larger Western supermarkets.

• *udon* – a very thick, white Japanese noodle with a square cross-section; served hot or cold. In its fresh form, it's known as *yude udon*. Found fresh, dried or frozen in packets in Japanese supermarkets, and fresh or dried in packets in larger Western supermarkets.

• *sōmen* – a thin, white Japanese noodle; usually served cold. Found dried in packets in Japanese and larger Western supermarkets.

• Shanghai noodle (*cui mian*) – a very thick, white Chinese noodle with a squarish cross-section. Found fresh in packets in oriental and Asian supermarkets. *Udon* (fresh or dried) can be substituted.

• *lamian* or *laghman* – a hand-pulled noodle from China and Central Asia; home-made by stretching, pulling and twisting sausages of dough.

• *misua* – a thread-like salted Chinese noodle. Found dried and fresh in packets in oriental and Asian supermarkets. Rice vermicelli can be substituted.

• *reshteh* – a flat, narrow, pale noodle from Central Asia; used in Persian and Afghani cuisine. Found dried in packets in Middle Eastern shops.

• standard thick wheat noodles – these are used across Asia where they are generally known by the Chinese names of *lo mein* (Cantonese), *lāo miàn* (Pinyin) and *lo mi* (Hokkien); called *gyohn khao swè* in Burma. Found dried, fresh or frozen in packets in oriental and Asian supermarkets, and dried and fresh in Western supermarkets. Can replace with medium egg noodles found fresh or dried in Western supermarkets (these are usually wheat noodles made with egg). I'm a fan of Sharwoods.

Rice Noodles

• broad, flat rice noodles – aka ribbon noodles, these are used across Asia where they are generally known by the Chinese names of *ho fun* and *chow fun* (Cantonese), *shahe fen* and *he fen* (Pinyin) and *hor fun* (Hokkien); called *sen yai* in Thailand and *hsan khao swè* in Burma. Think of them as the rice version of tagliatelle. Slightly chewy in texture. Found fresh, in strips or sheets that can be cut to the desired width, or dried in oriental and Asian supermarkets, and dried in larger Western supermarkets.

• narrow, flat rice noodles – aka rice sticks, these South-east Asian noodles are technically the same as *ho fun*, but narrower; called *bánh phở* in Vietnam and *sen lek* in Thailand. Found dried in large shrink-wrapped bundles in oriental and Asian supermarkets.

• *kway teow* – a flat, broad white noodle with a slightly chewy texture; used across Asia but mainly in Malaysia and Singapore; also known by its Chinese name *guotiao* (Pinyin), and called *guay tiew* in Thailand and *kwetiau* in Indonesia. Found fresh, in strips or sheets that can be cut to the desired width, or dried in large shrink-wrapped bundles in oriental and Asian supermarkets, and dried in larger Western supermarkets. Differs from *ho fun* in that *kway teow* is technically made from ricecakes sliced into strips (and is therefore slightly stiffer than *ho fun*), but interchangeable for most recipes.

• rice vermicelli noodles – thin, white South-east Asian noodles; known by their Chinese names of *mǐfěn* (Pinyin), *mai fun* (Cantonese), and *bee hoon* (Hokkien); called *bihun* in Indonesia and Malaysia, *bihon* in the Philippines, *sen mi* or *sen mee* in Thailand and *mohinga but* in Burma. Found fresh and dried in large shrink-wrapped bundles in oriental and Asian supermarkets and larger Western supermarkets.

• thick, round rice noodles – South-east Asian noodles; called *bún* in Vietnam, *mǐxiàn* in China, *meeshay but* in Burma and *laksa noodle* in Malaysia; also labelled confusingly as Chinese Guilin rice vermicelli. Think of them as the rice version of spaghetti. Found dried in large shrink-wrapped bundles in oriental and Asian supermarkets.

• rice flake noodle (*sen kuay chap*) – a big, flat Thai rice noodle shaped like a tortilla chip; also called triangle noodle. Occasionally found shaped as squares. Found dried in packets in oriental and Asian supermarkets. Curls up into rolls when cooked, hence also called 'rolled noodle'.

Buckwheat Noodles

• *naengmyeon* – a thin, grey, translucent Korean noodle; served cold. Found dried in large shrink-wrapped bundles in oriental and Asian supermarkets.
• *soba* – a thin, grey Japanese noodle with a square cross-section; served hot or cold. Found dried in packets in Japanese and larger Western supermarkets. Sometimes made with extra ingredients such as *matcha* (Japanese green tea).

Egg Noodles

• thin egg noodles (*you mian*) – yellow Chinese noodles made from a mixture of eggs and wheat flour; called *bakmi* in Malaysia and *bami* in Thailand. Found fresh or dried in packets in oriental and Asian supermarkets, and in larger Western supermarkets.
• thick egg noodles – pale yellow Chinese noodles with a square cross-section; known across Asia by the Chinese names of *yī miàn/yī fǔ miàn* (Pinyin), *yi mein/yee min/yee foo min/e-fu* (Cantonese), and *ee mee/ee foo mee* (Hokkien). Usually labelled as *yee mein* or *e-fu* in shops and restaurants. Chewy and slightly spongy, these are made from a mixture of eggs and wheat flour, fried and then dried. They can be found in bricks in oriental and Asian supermarkets.

Other Noodles

• glass noodles – thin, translucent noodles used across Asia; generally made from mung-bean starch (flour) but sometimes from other starches. Also known in English as cellophane noodles or crystal noodles. Glass noodles made of mung-bean starch are known as mung-bean thread noodles, bean thread noodles or mung-bean vermicelli in English, and are called *fěnsī* in China, *tanghoon* in Malaysia, *kyar-zun but* in Burma, *soun* or *suun* in Indonesia, *sotanghon* in the Philippines, *phing* or *fing* in Tibet, *bún tàu* or *bún tào* in Vietnam, and *woon sen* or *wun sen* in Thailand. *Dangmyeon* are Korean glass noodles made of sweet-potato starch; *harusame* are Japanese glass noodles made of potato starch; *miến or miến dong* are Vietnamese glass noodles made of canna lily starch. Glass noodles can be found dried in small and large shrink-wrapped bundles in oriental and Asian supermarkets.
• *hu tieu* – a flat, narrow, translucent noodle made from tapioca starch; used in Vietnamese and Cambodian dishes. Found dried in shrink-wrapped bundles in oriental and Asian supermarkets.

• *shirataki* or *konnyaku* – a thin, translucent, gelatinous Japanese noodle made from the root of the devil's tongue yam (aka elephant yam or konjac yam); '*shirataki*' means 'white waterfall'. So low in calories they're also known as zero noodles or miracle noodles. Found wet, packed in liquid, in Japanese and specialist stores. Some brands require rinsing or boiling before use.

READY-MADE STOCKS

There is absolutely nothing wrong with using shop-bought stock, either as a stock cube, as granules or in liquid form – just make sure you choose a low-sodium one if possible, as many are very salty. Nor is there anything wrong with using monosodium glutamate, or MSG (also known as VetSin and Accent). A few of the recipes use it, but if you are uncomfortable about this, feel free to use alternatives.

My favourite all-purpose stock base is Marigold bouillon, an almost magical powder that comes in a tub. It can be found in most supermarkets as well as healthfood stores.

Dashi granules, marvellous for whipping up Japanese dishes in an instant, can be found in sachets or tubs in Japanese supermarkets.

Knorr's pork and chicken granules are a wonderful cheat to add pep to Vietnamese dishes. These can be found in sachets or tubs in Vietnamese supermarkets.

SEASONINGS

I use certain condiments time and again. I'm quite picky about the brands I use and I strongly suggest you use the same ones:
• fish sauce: Viet Hoa Three Crabs
• light soy sauce: Pearl River Bridge Extra Virgin or Superior Light
• dark soy sauce: Pearl River Bridge Superior Dark
• Japanese soy sauce: Kikkoman
• Indonesian sweet soy sauce (*kecap manis*): Healthy Boy
• Yellow soybean sauce: Yeo's Salted Bean Sauce

CONDIMENTS AND GARNISHES

In Asia, the diner will always adjust the flavour of the noodles themselves according to preference. Generally a balance of salty, sour, spicy and sweet is expected. To this end, practically every dish is served with extra table condiments of some sort – for example, fish sauce and soy sauce for saltiness, fresh lime and vinegar for sourness, fresh and pickled chillies for spice and heat, and sugar for sweetness. Pickled chillies are easy to make (see page 12), but you can buy jars in oriental and Asian supermarkets. I'm also fond of a table condiment called Tean's Crispy Prawn Chilli, which provides salt, spice and savouriness (umami) in one hit. You can use it to top noodles or rice and even in sandwiches – and it's pretty addictive eaten straight from the jar.

Texture is also important, so extra garnishes will also be provided, such as beansprouts or fried shallots, crushed peanuts or crispy garlic. Fried shallots and crispy garlic are easy to make (see page 11), but you can buy jars and tubs in oriental and Asian supermarkets.

OILS

I use groundnut oil for all my cooking. It heats well, deep-fries beautifully, makes a good dressing, and has a clean neutral taste. If you're allergic to peanuts (which are the 'groundnuts' used to make the oil), feel free to substitute another neutral-flavoured vegetable oil that can be used for frying – for example, rapeseed oil or sunflower oil.

SPICES

Ground spices are fine for most of the recipes unless stated otherwise, but do bear in mind that they won't impart the same freshness as whole spices or those you grind yourself. Also remember that dried spices have a shelf life and will start to taste musty and stale after about 6 months to a year, so replace them when necessary.

If you can't get hold of the various ingredients that make up Chinese five spice, feel free to substitute a good-quality five spice powder. Bart's is the best brand in Western supermarkets, but any brand from an Asian or oriental supermarket will have the appropriate oomph.

BASIC STOCK RECIPES

Many, if not most, of the recipes in this book involve making a stock from scratch, but where they do not specify, feel free to cheat using the suggestions for ready-made stocks or make one of the stock recipes below.

Chicken stock

Makes about 1.5 litres

1kg chicken wings
1 onion, quartered (skin still on)
3cm knob of fresh root ginger, smashed (skin still on)
4 spring onions (with roots)
1 tsp salt
1 tbsp sugar
1 tsp cracked black peppercorns

Combine all the ingredients in a stockpot and add 2 litres water. Bring to the boil over a medium-high heat, then reduce the heat to medium-low. Partially cover the pan and simmer for 2 hours. Skim off any foam or scum that may rise to the top using a slotted spoon.

When the time is up, allow the stock to cool, then strain it through a fine-mesh sieve into a bowl or jug. If you want the chicken meat for a dish, pick it from the bones; discard the bones and remaining solids left in the sieve. The stock can be kept in the fridge for up to 3 days or frozen for up to 3 months.

Vegetable stock

Makes about 1.5 litres

2 onions, quartered (skin still on)
3 cloves garlic, bruised (skin still on)
3cm knob of fresh root ginger, smashed (skin still on)
4 spring onions (with roots)
4 dried shiitake mushrooms
2 celery sticks
6 white cabbage leaves
1 tsp salt
1 tbsp sugar
1 tsp cracked black peppercorns

Combine all the ingredients in a stockpot and add 2 litres water. Bring to the boil over a medium-high heat, then reduce the heat to medium-low. Partially cover the pan and simmer for 2 hours. Skim off any foam or scum that may rise to the top using a slotted spoon.

When the time is up, allow the stock to cool, then strain through a fine-mesh sieve into a bowl or jug, pressing down on the vegetables in the sieve to get as much liquid out as possible; discard the solids left in the sieve. The stock can be kept in the fridge for up to 3 days or frozen for up to 3 months.

Dashi

Makes about 1 litre

**50cm square sheet of dried kombu seaweed
handful of bonito flakes (katsuobushi)**

Put the seaweed in a saucepan, add 1 litre water and leave to soak for 20 minutes.

Bring to the boil, then immediately remove from the heat and scatter the bonito flakes over the surface of the water. Leave to steep for 3–4 minutes until the flakes sink to the bottom of the pan.

Strain through a fine sieve, coffee filter or tea strainer into a clean pan or jug. It's best to use dashi immediately, but you can keep it in a sealed container in the fridge for up to 4 days. Do not freeze.

PREPARATION AND COOKING TIMES

The preparation time (to make) for each recipe includes time spent chopping, stirring, mixing, assembling a dish and so on, when no heat is involved.

The cooking time refers to time when heat of any sort (hob and/or oven heat) is applied to the ingredients (such as frying, stir-frying, toasting, steaming, boiling, simmering, baking and so on) at any stage in the method.

SERVING QUANTITIES

Most dishes serve 2 people, but many are 'stock-pot' meals that will serve 4–6 people. A few are feasting dishes served on special occasions or meant for groups – these will serve 6–8 people.

RECIPES SUITABLE FOR FREEZING

In general, noodle dishes are unsuitable for freezing – certainly none of the noodles themselves or garnishes can be frozen once they've been prepared, so only make up the amount you will need for your meal.

However, the meat sauce, soup or gravy element in the following dishes can be frozen in an appropriate container for up to 3 months. When you want to serve, make sure you thaw the sauce fully before reheating it slowly in a saucepan.

- Chiang Mai Curry Noodles (*Khao Soi*), page 63
- Curry Laksa (*Laksa Lemak*), page 66
- Beef Noodle Soup (*Niu Rou Mian*), page 73
- Burmese Fish Chowder (*Mohinga*), page 74
- Coconut Chicken Noodles (*Ohn-No Khao Swè*), page 76
- Persian Noodle Soup (*Ash-e-Reshteh*), page 81
- Lamb and Vegetable Soup with Hand-pulled Noodles (*Laghman*), page 83
- Spicy Sichuan Noodles (*Dan Dan Mian*), page 90
- Beijing Bolognese (*Zha Jiang Mian*), page 98
- Pork and Rolled Noodle Stew (*Guay Jub / Kueh Chap / Kuay Jaab*), page 99
- Dai Meat and Tomato Noodles (*Kanom Jeen Nam Ngiao / Kao Soi Lao*), page 100
- Curry Udon (*Kare Udon*), page 104
- Mogok Round Rice Noodles (*Mogok Meeshay*), page 110
- Shan Noodles (*Shan Khao Swè*), page 111
- Mandalay Round Rice Noodles (*Mandalay Meeshay*), page 112
- Pork, Tomato, Kaffir Lime and Celery Noodles, page 117

EQUIPMENT

A stockpot, saucepan, wok, colander, sieve, ladle, slotted spoon and steamer are all the kitchen equipment you need.

CUTLERY AND CROCKERY

Most of the noodle dishes in this book are eaten using wooden chopsticks, apart from the following notable exceptions:

Korean noodle dishes are eaten using long, flat

metal chopsticks and a long-handled metal spoon.

Thai noodles served on a plate (eg *Pad Thai*, Ribbon Noodles with Gravy or Spicy Chicken and Glass Noodle Salad) are eaten using a matching metal fork and tablespoon. Thai noodles served in a bowl (eg Boat Noodle Soup or Pork and Rolled Noodle Stew) are eaten using wooden chopsticks and a Chinese spoon.

Burmese noodles are eaten using wooden chopsticks and a metal Chinese spoon unless the dish is soup-based (eg *Mohinga* or Smoky Mushroom and Glass Noodle Soup) when just the spoon will be used, known as a *mohinga* spoon, or where the dish is a salad (eg Rainbow Salad or Mandalay Hand-mixed Noodles) when the right hand will be used to eat. Incidentally, there's a Burmese saying that you'd serve your worst enemy glass noodles with a porcelain Chinese spoon – as a result we prefer the metal versions. Chopstick etiquette varies from country to country, but it's generally agreed that you shouldn't stick them in a bowl of food and leave them there, wave them around, make stabbing motions, cross them or use them to serve yourself from a communal dish.

As for crockery, deep noodle bowls or pasta plates will be appropriate for most dishes.

SECRET WEAPONS

You'll notice that some recipes call for 'secret weapons'. These are indispensable basic recipes which I turn to time and again, and which really do make all the difference for the recipes they feature in.

Black garlic oil (*mayu*)

Put 6 finely chopped garlic cloves, 4 tablespoons toasted sesame oil, 1 teaspoon golden caster sugar and 1 teaspoon salt in a small saucepan. Heat on medium-low heat, stirring occasionally, until the mix turns dark brown. At this point, reduce the heat to its lowest setting and leave to cook until the mix goes black. Transfer to a heatproof bowl and leave to cool, then blitz in a blender or food processor until completely smooth. The oil can be kept in a tightly covered jar or tub in the fridge for up to a week.

Braised pork belly (*cha shu*)

Place 1kg pork belly, rolled and tied, in a large saucepan. Add 250ml each sake and mirin, 125ml Japanese soy sauce (*shoyu*), 100ml apple juice, 100g golden caster sugar and enough water so the pork is submerged. Cover with a lid and bring to the boil. Move the lid slightly so there is a gap, turn the heat down to medium-low and leave to simmer gently for 3 hours until the pork is tender (when you poke it with a fork, this should slide in easily). Lift out the pork belly and cool, then slice into thin rounds; reserve the broth for another use. You can freeze the broth and any leftover pork at this stage for up to a month. However, it's better to freeze the pork before slicing into rounds, because it's easier to slice when it's still slightly frozen. Make sure you heat the pork slices through in piping hot broth before eating.

Burmese rice sauce (*gaw-yay*)

This is a type of thickener used to give a silky texture (*gaw-yay* literally means 'glue water') . In a small saucepan, whisk 2 tablespoons rice flour with 200ml cold water, then cook on a medium-high heat, continuing to whisk, for 5–6 minutes until it forms a translucent, silky sauce. Keep whisking, turn the heat to medium-low and simmer for another 15–20 minutes.

Burmese-style onion fritters (*kyet-thun kyaw*)

Slice 2 large onions and mix in a bowl with 60g self-raising flour, 30g glutinous rice flour, $1/2$ teaspoon salt, $1/4$ teaspoon MSG or 1 tablespoon Marigold bouillon powder and 50ml water. Heat a 5cm depth of oil in a wok on a medium-high heat. When you can feel waves of heat rising above with the palm of your hand, add 3 tablespoons of the onion mix to the hot oil, making sure each spoonful doesn't touch the others. Fry for 2–3 minutes, then flip and fry for another 2–3 minutes until golden brown all over. Scoop out with a slotted spoon and drain on kitchen paper. Fry the rest of the fritters in the same way. Serve at room temperature with the *Mohinga*, or piping hot as a snack.

Burmese water pickle (*yay tjin*)

This is served by all Mandalay *meeshay* sellers on the streets and is basically made from vegetable scraps. Whisk 2 tablespoons rice flour with enough cold water to form a runny paste. Chop the stems and leaves from a cauliflower (you could use the florets for Chicken and Cauliflower Noodles on page 84) and combine with the rice flour paste, plus 1 tablespoon salt, 1 teaspoon caster sugar and 1 tablespoon white vinegar. Mix thoroughly. Pack tightly in a sterilised jar and leave to ferment in the fridge for 5 days (or a cool, dark place for 3 days) before eating. The pickle can be kept for up to a week after fermenting.

Cabbage and Cucumber Salad

Thinly slice 8 white cabbage leaves and put into a bowl. Cut $\frac{1}{2}$ cucumber lengthways in half and scoop out the seeded centre, then cut the cucumber into julienne. Add to the bowl. Thinly slice 2 fresh red finger chillies and add to the bowl. Now add 1 teaspoon fish sauce, the juice of $\frac{1}{2}$ lime and a pinch of salt. Mix everything together, then allow the flavours to mellow for 15 minutes before serving.

Chilli oil

A common table condiment, this is available in jars in most supermarkets, but don't confuse with Western-style chilli oil which is simply oil infused with chillies. You can make your own as follows. Or make your own. Put 50g of chilli flakes in a heatproof container with a lid. Heat 200ml groundnut oil in a wok or frying pan on a high heat. When you can feel waves of heat coming from the top with the palm of your hand, pour the oil very carefully on to the chilli flakes. They will immediately sizzle and fizz as they fry in the oil. Leave to cool, then cover with the lid. The chilli oil can be kept in a cool, dark place for up to a week.

Chilli Soy Dip

Combine 4 fresh bird's eye chillies, sliced into rings; 4 tablespoons dark soy sauce; 2 tablespoons light soy sauce; 2 finely chopped garlic cloves; and the juice of 2 limes in a bowl. Leave for at least 15 minutes before serving so the flavours can mellow.

Crispy garlic oil

Peel the cloves from 2 bulbs of garlic and slice finely. Heat 6 tablespoons groundnut oil in a frying pan on a medium-low heat and stir-fry the garlic slices for 5–6 minutes until fragrant and golden brown. Leave to cool, then pour into a bowl and use immediately.

Crispy rice noodles

You need a small handful of dried (and uncooked) flat or round rice noodles. Heat a 5cm depth of vegetable oil in a wok or small frying pan over a high heat until hot, then break the noodles straight into the hot oil. They will puff up immediately like prawn crackers. As soon as they do, use a slotted spoon to fish them out and tip on to some kitchen paper to drain. Use as a garnish, or simply eat as a snack.

Deep-fried dried red chillies

Heat a 2cm depth of groundnut oil in a wok or deep frying pan on a medium-high heat until you can feel waves of heat coming off the oil with the palm of your hand. Add a handful of dried red chillies and let them sizzle for 4–5 minutes. Scoop them out and drain on kitchen paper. Allow to cool before using. The chillies can be kept in an airtight container in a cool, dark place for up to a week. Don't discard the oil, which is now infused with chilli flavour. Store the oil in a sterilised jar for up to a week and use as a garnish.

Fresh Chilli Garlic Sauce

Pound 150g fresh red finger chillies with 6 peeled garlic cloves and $\frac{1}{2}$ teaspoon salt in a pestle and mortar to make a smooth paste, or grind in a blender or food processor. Spoon the paste into a bowl or jug and whisk with 1 tablespoon caster sugar, 200ml white vinegar and 3 tablespoons hot water until the sugar dissolves. Serve immediately.

Fried dumpling skins

Take 16 dumpling or wonton skins and fold them in half. Heat 200ml groundnut oil in a wok or frying pan on a high heat. When you can feel waves of heat coming off the oil with the palm of your hand, add enough skins so you don't crowd the pan and deep-fry for 4–5 minutes until golden brown, turning them over halfway through. Scoop out with a slotted spoon and drain on kitchen paper. Repeat the process until you have fried all the skins. Leave to cool before using so they crisp up. The skins can be kept in an airtight container for up to a week.

Fried Peanuts

Heat 2 tablespoons groundnut oil in a frying pan on a medium heat and add 2 handfuls of raw peanuts, skin still on. Fry, tossing the peanuts with a spatula and shaking the pan, for 10 minutes until they smell fragrant and the skins become dark red and shiny. Remove from the heat. When the peanuts cool down, they should be good and crunchy. Use immediately or store them in an airtight container for up to a month.

Fried Shallots

While you can buy fried shallots in tubs in Asian and even Western supermarkets these days, it's quite satisfying to make your own. Heat a 1cm depth of groundnut oil in a wok on a high heat. When you can feel waves of heat rising with the palm of your hand, add 100g dried shallot or onion flakes. Turn the heat down to medium and fry, tossing occasionally, for 4–5 minutes until the shallots are golden brown. Drain on kitchen paper (reserve the cooled oil to dress salads or to drizzle on noodle soups) and leave to cool until crisp. The fried shallots can be stored in an airtight container for up to a month.

Hot Spring Eggs (*onsen tamago*)
In Japan, a raw egg is tipped into each bowl so it poaches only very lightly in the hot broth. If you're uncomfortable about eating nearly raw eggs, a hot spring egg (*onsen tamago*) is a lovely option – and one of my favourite ways of eating eggs. These are so-called because in Japan the eggs are traditionally cooked in hot springs, such as those in the foothills of Mount Fuji (*onsen* means 'hot spring' and *tamago* is 'egg'). The eggs are basically poached while still in their shells, but it's the lightest poach imaginable.

Without the luxury of a hot spring in your garden, this is the nearest you can get to a home-made *onsen* egg. Fill a small saucepan half-full with water (enough to submerge 4 eggs) and bring to the boil. Add 4 room-temperature eggs, then immediately remove from the heat and cover with a lid. Leave the eggs for 7 minutes before cracking them open – the yolk should still be runny and the white barely cooked (you may need to tweak the time depending on the size of your eggs).

Lard Pieces in Lard Oil
Rinse 200g pork belly fat and pat dry with kitchen paper. Cut the fat into 1cm cubes using a sharp knife or kitchen scissors. Heat a wok or large frying pan on a medium-high heat and add the cubes in one layer. The fat will melt out and the cubes will fry in this rendered oil. Flip the cubes from time to time to brown evenly. When they become light brown all over, remove the wok from the heat – the cubes will continue to cook in the hot oil. As soon as they become golden brown, the lard pieces are ready to use. You can store the lard pieces and lard oil separately for up to a week, with the lard pieces in an airtight container in the fridge and the lard oil in a covered dish at room temperature. Or you can store the lard pieces with the oil in an airtight container for 1 week at room temperature.

Indonesian Chilli Paste (*sambal oelek*)
Remove the stalks, seeds and white pith from 6 fresh red finger chillies, then dice the chillies into 1cm squares. Place in a pestle and mortar with $^1/_4$ teaspoon salt and pound with a circular grinding motion to make as smooth a paste as you can manage. Scoop the chilli paste into a bowl. Add another $^1/_4$ teaspoon salt and the juice of $^1/_2$ lime (or 1 tablespoon rice vinegar) and stir well. Serve immediately or keep in the fridge in an airtight container for up to a fortnight.

Onion and Tomato Salad
This salad is always eaten with fried noodles in Burma. Shave slices from a peeled medium onion as thinly as possible. Soak them in cold water for 30 minutes, then drain and mix in a bowl with a thinly sliced ripe tomato (juice, seeds and all), 1 tablespoon lemon juice and $^1/_4$ teaspoon salt. A dirtier version of this salad is made by mixing the onion with 3 tablespoons tomato ketchup. It's heavenly.

Pickled Chillies
Thinly slice 4 fresh red finger chillies and mix with 4 tablespoons rice vinegar or cider vinegar, 1 tablespoon caster sugar and $^1/_2$ teaspoon salt. Store in a sterilised jar and use within a month.

Pickled Garlic
Garlic in Thailand and Burma is much sweeter and smaller than that sold in the UK, with papery pink skin that you can eat. The garlic is normally pickled as whole bulbs, skin, stem and all. When making this recipe using regular garlic in this country, you should still keep the skin on because the skin adds to the flavour and helps the garlic stay firm and crunchy. But when you come to eat, you should probably remove the skin.

Wash 6 bulbs of garlic thoroughly in cold water but do not peel. In a saucepan, combine 125ml rice vinegar, 4 tablespoons caster sugar, 1 tablespoon salt and 100ml water and bring to a rolling boil. After a minute, turn the heat down to medium and simmer for 5–6 minutes until reduced to a thin syrup. Remove from the heat, add the garlic and leave to cool. Once cold, pour everything into a sterilised jar or container (making sure the garlic bulbs are covered by the pickle) and leave in the fridge for at least a week before using. The pickled garlic can be kept in the fridge for about 6 months.

Ramen eggs (*nitamago*)
To make 6 ramen eggs, whisk 3 tablespoons each light soy sauce, dark soy sauce and mirin or dry sherry

with 1 teaspoon caster sugar and $^1/_2$ teaspoon instant dashi (or 1 tablespoon Marigold bouillon powder or $^1/_4$ teaspoon MSG) in a small bowl or jug. Set to one side. Now soft-boil 6 room-temperature eggs: place them in a saucepan that just fits them and add water to cover. Bring to the boil, then turn the heat to medium and simmer for 4 minutes. Remove from the heat and run cold water over the eggs to stop them cooking any further. As soon as they are cool enough to touch, peel them very carefully, making sure you don't split the whites. Place the peeled eggs in a large re-sealable plastic bag and pour the soy marinade on top. Roll the eggs around in the marinade, then close the bag tightly. Place the bag of eggs in a bowl and leave in the fridge overnight (turn them once for even coverage). Before using, drain the eggs, pat them dry and slice in half. This recipe will make more than you need, but ramen eggs are an excellent snack mashed on to rice or toast.

Tamarind Juice

Many recipes call for tamarind juice or tamarind water, which is made from a block of pure tamarind that you can buy in Asian and oriental supermarkets. For tamarind juice, soak a 2.5cm cube of tamarind in 200ml just-boiled water until the tamarind pulp breaks down into the liquid (this will take at least 30 minutes), then strain the dark brown, opaque juice. This will make more tamarind juice than most recipes need, but you can freeze any that you don't use in an ice cube tray to use at a later date. Note that tamarind paste in jars is very sweet and often mixed with other ingredients. If you must use it to make tamarind juice, adjust accordingly by tasting and reducing the amount of any sugar and salt you use in the main recipe.

Tempura Crumbs (*tenkasu*)

Sift 120g plain flour and $^1/_2$ teaspoon bicarbonate of soda into a bowl and make a well in the centre. Add a beaten egg and 250ml iced water. Whisk everything lightly with chopsticks 3 or 4 times (for no more than 5 seconds). The batter is meant to be lumpy. Heat a 5cm depth of groundnut oil in a wok on a medium-high heat. Have a wire rack ready to drain your tempura. When you can feel waves of heat coming off the top of the wok with the palm of your hand, use a whisk, bamboo wok brush or 2 pairs of chopsticks to drip the batter into the oil like raindrops. These should immediately form small, crispy tempura pieces in the hot oil. Don't crowd the pan – you should make several batches. Scoop out the tempura pieces with a slotted spoon before they burn and drain them on kitchen paper. If they clump together, you can break them into pieces once they are cool. Use as soon as they have cooled completely. This will make a large quantity, much more than you need for the recipe, but tempura crumbs can be frozen and are an excellent crispy topping for any noodle dish.

Tonkatsu sauce

Similar to barbecue sauce, this fruity brown sauce adds an essential tangy dimension to any dish. You can buy it ready-made – the brand that everyone uses is Bulldog, which you can get from Japanese supermarkets – or make your own. Mix together 6 tablespoons tomato ketchup, 4 tablespoons dark soy sauce, 1 tablespoon each Worcestershire sauce, golden caster sugar and pomegranate syrup or apple sauce (optional), and 1 teaspoon each yellow American mustard, ground ginger and garlic powder. Dilute with enough hot water to get a consistency like thin honey.

Vietnamese dipping sauce (*nước chấm*)

Grind 2 peeled garlic cloves with $^1/_2$ teaspoon salt in a pestle and mortar, adding 4 fresh red finger chillies or 2 fresh red bird's eye chillies one by one (remove the stalks), to make a coarse paste. Alternatively, grind the garlic, salt and chillies together in a blender or food processor. Transfer the paste to a small bowl and add 4 tablespoons each rice vinegar and fish sauce, 2 tablespoons each boiling water and caster sugar, and the juice of a lime. Whisk well until the sugar has dissolved. Set aside to allow the flavours to mellow for 5 minutes before serving. Use the same day.

Yellow split-pea crackers (*hbè gyun kyaw*)

These make a brilliant snack as well as an excellent garnish for *Mohinga* and *Yakhine Mohntee* (Rakhine Noodles). Soak 100g dried yellow split peas overnight in cold water, then drain well and mix in a bowl with 85g plain flour, 60g glutinous rice flour, $^1/_2$ teaspoon each bicarbonate of soda and salt, $^1/_2$ teaspoon MSG (optional) and 400ml water. Heat a 5cm depth of oil in a wok on a medium-high heat. When you can feel waves of heat coming off the top with the palm of your hand, add a ladle of batter to the hot oil, in a swirl so it forms a round cracker. Fry for 3–4 minutes, then flip the cracker and fry for another 3–4 minutes until both sides are golden brown. Carefully lift out the cracker and drain on kitchen paper. Make the rest of the crackers in the same way. When cool, break into small pieces.

STIR-FRIES

Chicken chow mein

(China)

Chow mein is just the Chinese term for 'fried noodles', so it's not surprising that there are countless variations. Wholeheartedly adopted overseas, and often the default order from a takeaway menu, it's so easy to make your own version at home. Your stomach will thank you for it, as the home-made version is much less likely to be greasy.

Serves 2 | Takes 20 minutes to make, 12 minutes to cook

200g fresh standard thick wheat noodles (*lo mein*) or 125g dried, or you can use medium egg noodles
2 skinless, boneless chicken thighs, about 250g total weight, cut into small strips
3 tbsp groundnut oil
4 cloves garlic, finely chopped
100g mangetouts, julienned
1 large carrot, julienned
2 tbsp light soy sauce
1 tbsp dark soy sauce
1 tbsp oyster sauce
1 tbsp toasted sesame oil
1 tsp golden caster sugar
1 tsp white pepper
100g beansprouts, topped and tailed
2 spring onions (green and white parts), sliced diagonally into rings

For the marinade
1 tsp light soy sauce
1 tsp cornflour
1 tbsp Chinese rice wine or dry sherry
1/2 tsp white pepper

Prepare the noodles according to the packet instructions. Set aside.

Mix together the marinade ingredients in a bowl. Add the chicken and turn to coat, then set aside to marinate for 10 minutes.

Heat a wok or deep frying pan on a high heat until you can feel the waves of heat coming from it with the palm of your hand. Add the groundnut oil to the wok followed by the garlic and stir-fry for a couple of minutes until fragrant.

Add the chicken and stir-fry for 2–3 minutes until it loses its translucency (it will be cooked outside but not yet inside), then add the mangetouts and carrot. Keep the heat high and stir-fry for another minute.

Add the noodles, soy sauces, oyster sauce, sesame oil, sugar, white pepper and 2 tablespoons cold water. Stir and toss everything for a couple more minutes, then add the beansprouts and spring onions and stir again to incorporate. Serve immediately in pasta dishes, with chopsticks.

Cook's tip
You can use pretty much any vegetables you have to hand – try cabbage, peppers or mushrooms – as long as you cut them into similar-sized pieces so they will cook in the same time. You could also use ham or peeled prawns instead of chicken, or keep it entirely vegetarian and add strips of omelette instead.

Shanghai fried noodles

(Hong Kong)

Shanghai Fried Noodles are popular in both Hong Kong and in the West, but it seems that, like the Indian balti, the dish was invented by enterprising chefs abroad rather than born in Shanghai itself. The dish is usually made with fresh Shanghai noodles, which you can buy in Chinese supermarkets, but you can use fresh *udon* noodles (*yude udon*) instead, as they're similar and much easier to find.

Serves 4 | Takes 25 minutes to make, 15 minutes to cook

200g beef flank steak, sliced
    into strips
400g fresh Shanghai noodles
    (*cui mian*)
groundnut oil

For the meat marinade
1 tbsp hoisin sauce
1 tbsp Chinese rice wine or
    dry sherry
1 tsp cornflour
1 tsp white pepper

For the stir-fry
4 cloves garlic, finely chopped
2cm knob of fresh root ginger,
    peeled and finely chopped
200g Chinese leaf, shredded
50ml chicken stock
2 tbsp dark soy sauce
1 tbsp light soy sauce
1 tbsp oyster sauce
1 tbsp toasted sesame oil

Combine the marinade ingredients in a bowl and whisk thoroughly. Add the meat and leave to marinate for 20 minutes.

Meanwhile, blanch the noodles by putting them in a bowl, pouring just-boiled water over them and leaving them for 5 minutes. Drain, then toss with 1 teaspoon groundnut oil to prevent them from sticking together.

Heat 2 tablespoons groundnut oil in a wok or deep frying pan on a high heat. Add the marinated meat and stir-fry for 5 minutes until cooked through. Empty the contents of the wok into a dish and set to one side.

Heat another tablespoon of groundnut oil in the wok, still on a high heat. Stir-fry the garlic and ginger for a couple of minutes, then add the Chinese leaf. Return the cooked meat to the wok along with the stock and stir-fry for 5 minutes.

Now add the noodles to the wok plus the soy sauces, oyster sauce and sesame oil. Stir and toss everything for 2 more minutes. Divide among 4 pasta dishes and serve immediately, with chopsticks and Chinese spoons.

Cook's Tip
Shanghai fried noodles are usually made with beef, but pork and chicken can also be used. A leafy green vegetable is a must – here I've used Chinese leaf, but pak choi would be just as good.

Singapore noodles

(Hong Kong)

There's no debate about one aspect of the origin of these noodles – they are certainly not from Singapore, and if you even suggest it to a native Singaporean (such as my friends who run the Plus Six Five supper-club), they get ever so slightly vexed. It's suspected that Singapore Noodles were invented in Hong Kong or even by Chinese immigrants in the US. Wherever they come from, they're delicious and a popular item on any takeaway menu, but easy to make at home yourself.

Serves 2 | Takes 20 minutes to make, 20 minutes to cook

100g skinless, boneless chicken thighs, sliced into strips
100g peeled large, raw prawns, deveined and cut crossways in half
150g dried rice vermicelli noodles
5–6 tbsp groundnut oil
2 eggs, beaten
2 tbsp Madras curry powder
1 medium onion, sliced
1 red pepper, deseeded and sliced
100g beansprouts, topped and tailed
100g Chinese barbecue pork (*char siu*), sliced into strips (optional)
4 spring onions (green and white parts), sliced diagonally
sprigs of fresh coriander, to garnish

For the chicken and prawn marinade
1cm piece of fresh root ginger, peeled and finely chopped
1 tbsp cornflour
2 tbsp Chinese rice wine or dry sherry
1 tbsp light soy sauce
1 tsp golden caster sugar
$\frac{1}{2}$ tsp salt
$\frac{1}{2}$ tsp freshly ground white pepper

For the sauce
50ml hot chicken stock
1 tbsp Indonesian sweet soy sauce (*kecap manis*)
1 tsp golden caster sugar
1 tsp salt
1 tsp freshly ground white pepper

Combine the chicken and prawns with the marinade ingredients in a bowl. Leave to marinate for 20 minutes. Whisk the sauce ingredients together in another smaller bowl and set to one side.

Put the noodles into a heatproof bowl. Pour over plenty of just-boiled water and untangle the noodles with a fork, then leave to soak for 5 minutes. Drain in a colander and rinse with running cold water. Set to one side in the colander so that any residual water can continue to drain.

Heat 2 tablespoons oil in a wok or large frying pan on a medium heat. Add the beaten egg and move the pan around to spread the egg out evenly into a thin omelette. When the omelette is firm all the way through and golden on the base, use a spatula to ease around its edges and flip the omelette over.

Cook for a further 1–2 minutes until golden on both sides. Transfer the omelette to a plate and let it cool, then slice into strips before setting aside.

Heat another tablespoon of oil in the wok on medium-high heat. Add the marinated chicken and prawns and stir-fry for 4–5 minutes until the chicken is cooked and the prawns have turned pink. Scoop them out into a dish and set aside.

Add 2–3 tablespoons more oil to the wok and heat on a high heat for a minute. Now turn the heat down to medium, add the curry powder and swirl the spiced oil in the wok for 30 seconds until fragrant.

Next add the onion and stir-fry for 1–2 minutes until starting to soften. Add the red pepper and stir-fry for 2–3 minutes, then tip in the beansprouts and stir-fry for a further 1–2 minutes.

Finally, add the noodles, cooked chicken and prawns, omelette strips, barbecue pork (if using) and spring onions. Using chopsticks or tongs, toss the ingredients to combine, then drizzle the sauce over them. Toss a few more times to ensure even distribution and that everything is heated through, then dish up on to 2 plates. Garnish with coriander and serve with forks.

Beef with Ribbon Noodles

Beef Chow Fun (Hong Kong)

Beef Chow Fun is a Cantonese classic served in dim sum restaurants and teahouses throughout Hong Kong. '*Wok hei*' is vital in making this dish – the 'essence' imparted by a hot wok during stir-frying. This means the cooking must be quick and over a high heat – ideally a gas flame.

Serves 4 | Takes 25 minutes to make, 8 minutes to cook

For the stir-fry
250g flank steak, cut into thin 2.5cm-long slices across the grain
400g fresh broad, flat rice noodles (*ho fun*) or 150g dried
2 tbsp groundnut oil
4 cloves garlic, chopped
2cm knob of fresh root ginger, peeled and julienned
1 medium onion, sliced
100g beansprouts, topped and tailed
2 spring onions (green and white parts), sliced lengthways and then cut across into 5cm pieces

For the beef marinade
1 tsp bicarbonate of soda
1 tbsp cornflour
1 tsp caster sugar
1/2 tsp white pepper
1 tbsp Chinese rice wine or dry sherry
1 tbsp light soy sauce
1 tbsp toasted sesame oil

For the noodle sauce
50ml beef stock
1 tbsp fermented black beans, finely chopped
1 tbsp light soy sauce
1 tbsp dark soy sauce
1 tsp toasted sesame oil
1 tsp caster sugar

1 tsp white pepper

Toss the beef with the bicarbonate of soda to coat, then leave for 5 minutes. Rinse thoroughly with cold water and pat dry. Mix the beef with the remaining marinade ingredients in a bowl, then set aside for at least 15 minutes.

If using fresh *ho fun* noodles, carefully separate them (they should come apart in 2.5cm strands), then set them aside, lightly covered with a damp cloth or clingfilm. If using dried *ho fun*, put them in a large heatproof bowl and generously cover with just-boiled water. After a minute, untangle the noodles, then leave them to soak for a further 6 minutes until al dente. Drain in a colander and rinse thoroughly under running cold water. Set to one side in the colander so that any residual water can continue to drain.

Heat a wok on a high heat until you can feel the waves of heat coming from it with the palm of your hand ('*wok hei*'). Add the oil to the wok followed by the garlic and ginger and stir fry for 2–3 minutes until fragrant.

Add the marinated beef and stir-fry for another couple of minutes before adding the onion and stir-frying for 2–3 minutes until

it is translucent.

Next add the noodles, beansprouts, spring onions and the noodle sauce ingredients. Being gentle so you don't break the noodles, toss everything together for 2–3 minutes until piping hot. Divide among 4 pasta plates and serve immediately, with chopsticks.

Cook's Tip
Don't be heavy-handed when tossing the ingredients in the wok, or with the amount of oil you use, as this will result in the sort of claggy mess you find in some restaurants and takeaways!

Spicy Fried Noodles

Mie Goreng (Malaysia/Indonesia/Singapore)

Mie Goreng (also *Bakmi* or *Bami Goreng*, *Mee Goreng* or *Mi Goreng* – all of which just mean 'fried noodles') is a dish common in Malaysia and Singapore but found everywhere in Indonesia, from high-end restaurants to street stalls. If you're a fan of instant noodles, *Mie Goreng* flavour is always a winner with its spicy fried taste (people have been known to buy boxes of the Indomie brand on eBay). Or you could just make your own using the recipe below.

Serves 2–3 | Takes 20 minutes to make, 12 minutes to cook

150g dried thin egg noodles (*bakmi*) or 250g fresh
4 tbsp groundnut oil
3 cloves garlic, finely chopped
2cm knob of fresh root ginger, peeled and finely chopped
1 skinless, boneless chicken thigh, about 100g, cut into small strips
8 raw king prawns, peeled and deveined
1 stick Chinese celery, finely chopped
1 large tomato, quartered
4 tbsp Indonesian sweet soy sauce (*kecap manis*)
100g beansprouts, topped and tailed
100g choy sum, sliced
1 tbsp dark soy sauce
1 tbsp light soy sauce

For the spice paste (*rempah*)
6 Asian shallots or 1 banana shallot, peeled
4 candlenuts or macadamia nuts, toasted
1 tsp white peppercorns
3 dried red chillies, soaked in warm water and drained
2 large, fresh red chillies
1 tsp salt

To serve
2 eggs
4 garlic chives, cut into 2.5cm pieces
2 spring onions (green and white parts), finely sliced
chilli sauce (sriracha is particularly good)

If using dried noodles, prepare according to the packet instructions but reduce the cooking time slightly so that the noodles are al dente rather than tender. If using fresh noodles, they need no prep before adding to the wok (they are already al dente).

Grind the spice paste ingredients together to a smooth paste using a pestle and mortar, a blender or a food processor.

Heat 3 tablespoons oil in a wok or deep frying pan on a high heat and stir-fry the spice paste for 30 seconds until fragrant. Add the garlic and ginger to the wok and stir-fry for 2–3 minutes until they are fragrant.

Add the chicken and prawns and toss to mix into the spice paste, then stir-fry for 2 minutes until the chicken is opaque. Now turn the heat down to medium. Add the Chinese celery, tomato, sweet soy sauce and 100ml water and mix well. Cook for 5 minutes until the liquid has reduced and thickened.

Meanwhile, fry the eggs in a separate pan in the remaining groundnut oil, then set to one side.

Turn the heat under the wok back to high and add the noodles, beansprouts, choy sum and soy sauces. Stir and toss to combine, then stir-fry for 2–3 more minutes.

Dish up into 2 pasta dishes and top each serving with a fried egg. Sprinkle with garlic chives and spring onions and serve immediately, with chopsticks and chilli sauce on the side.

Seafood Ribbon Noodles

Char Kway Teow (Malaysia/Indonesia/Singapore)

Considered one of the national dishes of Singapore, this is also a popular street-hawker dish in Indonesia, Malaysia and Brunei. Traditionally it is stir-fried in lard, and topped with an unusual type of cockle bursting with dark red juices known as a blood cockle, but I've used groundnut oil to be a bit healthier, and normal cockles as you can't get blood cockles in the UK for love or money. Just as for Beef Chow Fun, '*wok hei*' is important for this dish – in fact, I recommend cooking each portion separately to ensure optimum flavour and texture.

Serves 2 | Takes 20 minutes to make, 8 minutes to cook

200g fresh broad, flat rice noodles (*ho fun*) or 75g dried
8 tbsp groundnut oil
2 cloves garlic, finely chopped
1 Chinese sausage (*lap cheong*), thinly sliced at an angle
50g ready-made fishcake, sliced into strips
8 large raw prawns, peeled and deveined
50g beansprouts, topped and tailed
2 tbsp light soy sauce
2 tsp dark soy sauce
2 tsp Indonesian sweet soy sauce (*kecap manis*)
2 tsp chilli sauce (sriracha is particularly good)
2 eggs
2 garlic chives, cut into 5cm lengths
100g shelled fresh cockles
white pepper to taste

If using fresh *ho fun* noodles, carefully separate them (they should come apart in 2.5cm strands), then set them aside, lightly covered with a damp cloth or clingfilm. If using dried *ho fun*, put them in a large heatproof bowl and generously cover with just-boiled water. After a minute, untangle the noodles, then leave them to soak for a further 6 minutes until al dente. Drain in a colander and rinse thoroughly under running cold water. Set to one side in the colander so that any residual water can continue to drain.

You need to cook this one portion at a time for the best results:

Heat a wok on a high heat until you can feel the waves of heat coming from it with the palm of your hand ('*wok hei*'). Add 2 tablespoons oil, half the garlic and half the Chinese sausage, and stir-fry for 1–2 minutes until the garlic is fragrant and the sausage is glossy. With the heat still on high, add half the fish cake and 4 prawns, and stir-fry for another couple of minutes until the prawns turn pink.

Turn the heat down to medium and push everything to the side of the wok, then add half of the noodles and beansprouts, half of all the sauces and 3 tablespoons water to the cleared space. Mix these new ingredients together, then stir-fry for 2 minutes in the cleared space.

Now push everything to the side of the wok again. Add 2 tablespoons oil to the cleared space and, when it's hot, crack in an egg. Break up the egg with your spatula, then pull everything back into the centre of the wok and combine well with the egg.

Next add half the chives and white pepper to taste and stir-fry to combine well. Lastly, add half of the cockles and stir-fry for 30 seconds. Serve immediately on a plate, with chopsticks. Repeat the process for the other portion.

Fried Hokkien Prawn Noodles

Hokkien Hae Mee (Singapore)

Hokkien Mee are noodles cooked in the Hokkien style, which means from the Fujian province of China. Fujian immigrants introduced two main types of noodle to South-east Asia: *Hokkien Hae Mee* (with prawns) and *Hokkien Char Mee* (fried). *Hokkien Hae Mee* itself comes in two different forms – stir-fried and in a soup. This is a recipe for the stir-fried version, popular in Singapore.

Serves 2 | Takes 1 hour to make, 1 hour 30 minutes to cook

100g dried thick, round rice noodles (Vietnamese *bún* or Guilin rice vermicelli)
150g fresh thin egg noodles (*bakmi*) or 75g dried
200g raw medium prawns (in shell, with heads)
4 tbsp groundnut oil
500ml vegetable or chicken stock
1 tbsp fish sauce
1 tsp caster sugar
1 x 100g piece of pork belly
100g raw squid rings
4 cloves garlic, finely chopped
2 eggs, beaten
1 tbsp light soy sauce
100g ready-made fishcake, sliced
50g beansprouts, topped and tailed
4 garlic chives, chopped
1 tsp freshly ground white pepper

For the garnish
Lard Oil (see Secret Weapon below)
Indonesian Chilli Paste (Secret Weapons, page 12)
lime wedges

Put the rice noodles in a large heatproof bowl and generously cover with just-boiled water. Leave to soak for 45 minutes until pliable. Drain in a colander and rinse thoroughly with running cold water, then set to one side in the colander so that any residual water can continue to drain.

If using dried egg noodles, prepare according to the packet instructions but reduce the cooking time slightly so that the noodles are al dente rather than tender. If using fresh noodles, they need no prep before adding to the wok (they are already al dente).

Peel the prawns, keeping the tails on, and devein them; set aside. Do not discard the heads or shells. Heat 2 tablespoons oil in a wok or large frying pan on a medium-high heat. Add the prawn heads and shell and stir-fry for 5–6 minutes until they turn pink and smell fragrant. Remove the wok from the heat.

Combine the stock with 250ml water in a saucepan. Tip the fried prawn heads and shells into the pan (don't wash the wok yet) and bring to the boil. Add the fish sauce and sugar. Reduce the heat to medium and simmer for 30 minutes.

Add the pork belly to the saucepan and simmer for 45 minutes until tender. Scoop the pork out with a slotted spoon and leave to cool, then chop into bite-size pieces.

Strain the broth into a clean saucepan; discard the prawn heads and shells. Bring the broth back to the boil. Add the prawns and squid rings and let them bubble away for 30–45 seconds until cooked. Scoop them out with a slotted spoon and set to one side with the pork.

Now put the wok back on a medium-high heat and add the remaining 2 tablespoons oil. Fry the garlic for 2–3 minutes until fragrant. Scoop to one side of the wok; add the beaten eggs to the other side and scramble them. Turn the heat up to high and add the rice noodles and the egg noodles. Sprinkle over the soy sauce and toss well to mix, then stir-fry for 2–3 minutes.

Ladle half the broth from the saucepan into the wok. Reduce the heat to medium, cover the wok with a lid and allow everything to braise in the broth for 3–4 minutes. Remove the lid and add the pork belly, fishcake and the rest of the broth. Turn the heat back up to high, toss again and fry for 4–5 minutes until some of the broth has been absorbed by the noodles.

Reduce the heat to medium once more. Add the prawns and squid, the beansprouts, garlic chives and white pepper and fry for a final 1–2 minutes. Serve immediately on pasta plates, with chopsticks and with lard oil, *sambal oelek* and lime wedges on the side.

Tamarind and Garlic Chive Noodles

Pad Thai (Thailand)

Pad Thai, or *Phat Thai*, is actually thought to have been introduced by Vietnamese traders to the Thai capital of Ayutthaya in the 1700s. The dish was made popular in Thailand by Luang Phibunsongkhram, when he was prime minister in 1930s to 40s: it was given its name as part of his campaign to promote Thai nationalism, and to reduce domestic rice consumption. Nowadays, it is one of the best-loved dishes of Thailand.

Serves 4 | Takes 15 minutes to make, 12 minutes to cook

400g fresh broad, flat rice noodles (*ho fun*) or 150g dried
4 tbsp Tamarind Juice (Secret Weapons, page 13)
50ml fish sauce
50g palm sugar or soft dark brown sugar
1 tsp chilli flakes
8 tbsp groundnut oil
1 tbsp dried shrimps
2 cloves garlic, finely chopped
100g firm tofu, cut into 1cm cubes
8 raw king prawns, peeled (tail left on) and deveined
2 large eggs
25g preserved radish, finely chopped
small handful of dry-roasted peanuts, finely chopped
100g beansprouts, topped and tailed

6 garlic chives, cut into 2.5cm pieces

To garnish
lime wedges
chilli flakes
fish sauce

If using fresh *ho fun*, carefully separate the noodles (they should come apart in 2.5cm strands) and set them aside, lightly covered with a damp cloth or clingfilm. If using dried *ho fun*, put them in a large heatproof bowl and generously cover with just-boiled water. After a minute, untangle the noodles, then leave them to soak for a further 3 minutes until just pliable (ie bend rather than snap). Drain in a colander and rinse thoroughly under running cold water. Set to one side in the colander so that any residual water can continue to drain.

Combine the tamarind juice, fish sauce, sugar and chilli flakes in a small saucepan and heat on a medium heat for 5–6 minutes until the sugar dissolves. Set to one side.

Heat 4 tablespoons oil in a wok or deep frying pan on a high heat until it sizzles. Add the dried shrimps and stir-fry for a minute until fragrant. Add the garlic and stir fry for another 30 seconds until fragrant but not brown. Add the noodles with 2 tablespoons water and stir-fry for 2–3 minutes until the water evaporates. Next add the tamarind/fish sauce mix and stir-fry for 5 minutes until the noodles are al dente.

Push the noodles to the side of the wok and add the remaining 4 tablespoons oil to the cleared space. With the heat still on high, fry the tofu and prawns for 2–3 minutes in the cleared space until the prawns turn pink. Push to the side to join the noodles, then crack the eggs into the vacated space and scramble quickly.

Mix everything together gently, then add the radish, peanuts, beansprouts and chives. Stir-fry for a minute until everything is combined and piping hot, then serve immediately on pasta plates, with forks and spoons. Serve the garnishes on the side for people to help themselves.

Crispy Noodles

Mi Krop (Thailand)

Mi Krop, or *Mee Grob*, is a Thai dish whose name literally means 'crisp noodles'. Doused with a sweet, sour and salty sauce just before serving, it's a beautiful balance of texture and flavours.

Serves 2 | Takes 40 minutes to make, 20 minutes to cook

200g dried rice vermicelli noodles
groundnut oil, for deep-frying
125g extra-firm tofu, cut into 2.5cm cubes
handful of dried shrimps
3 cloves garlic, finely chopped
3 Asian shallots, finely chopped
200g minced pork
12 raw king prawns, peeled and deveined
2 eggs, beaten
100g beansprouts, topped and tailed

For the sauce
4 tbsp Tamarind Juice (see Secret Weapons, page 13)
2 tbsp tomato purée
2 tbsp palm sugar or soft dark brown sugar
2 tbsp fish sauce
1 tbsp lime juice
1 tbsp yellow soybean sauce
1 tsp chilli flakes

For the garnish
4 spring onions (green and white parts), cut into 2.5cm pieces
2 garlic chives, cut into 2.5cm pieces
handful of fresh coriander leaves, chopped
2 bulbs Pickled Garlic (Secret Weapons, page 12), thinly sliced
2 fresh red finger chillies, deseeded and thinly sliced

Put the dried vermicelli in a colander and quickly rinse with cold water, then shake as dry as possible. Leave to drain and dry in the colander for 30 minutes. Loosen the noodles with your fingers – they should be nicely pliable now.

While the noodles are drying, pour a 7.5cm depth of oil into a wok and heat on a high heat. When the oil is hot (you'll feel waves of heat coming off if you hold your palm above it), turn the heat down to medium. Add the tofu and deep-fry for a couple of minutes until golden brown. Remove the fried tofu with a slotted spoon and drain it on kitchen paper.

If the level of oil has dropped in the wok, top it up so there's a 7.5cm depth again, and turn the heat back up to high.

Make sure the rice vermicelli noodles are completely dry, then test-fry a noodle in the oil to see if it's hot enough. If the noodle puffs up, the oil is ready. Put one bundle of vermicelli into the hot oil – it should puff up and expand immediately. As soon as it does, flip the bundle over and fry the other side for a few seconds, then remove and drain on kitchen paper. Fry the rest of the noodle bundles in the same manner and drain, then set aside.

Turn off the heat. Pick up the wok and carefully pour most of the oil away into a heatproof container, leaving about 2 tablespoons in the wok (once cold, you can store the oil in a lidded container for reuse later).

Put the wok back on the heat and turn it to medium. Fry the dried shrimps, garlic and shallots for 2–3 minutes until fragrant, then add the pork and stir-fry for 3–4 minutes until cooked, breaking up any clumps. Lastly add the prawns and stir-fry for 2 minutes until opaque.

Scoop everything to the side of the wok. Turn the heat up to high and add 1 tablespoon of the oil you poured away earlier to the cleared space. Add the beaten eggs to this space and scramble them. Then add the beansprouts and toss everything together. Fry for another minute. Tip the contents of the wok into a dish and set to one side.

Now turn the heat to medium-low and add another tablespoon of the poured-away oil. Add all the sauce ingredients and mix thoroughly, then simmer for 10 minutes until the sauce thickens to a thin syrup. Turn the heat down to low and return the pork/prawn/egg mix to the wok as well as the deep-fried tofu. Mix together so everything is coated with the sauce.

Finally, add the crispy noodles and toss gently to make sure they are coated with the sauce. Transfer to a serving platter and garnish with the spring onions, garlic chives, coriander, pickled garlic and chillies. Serve immediately while the noodles are still crisp – give people plates and forks and spoons to help themselves.

Fried Festival Noodles

Yakisoba (Japan)

In Japan it's almost always festival time. In the summer, everyone dresses up in special kimonos known as *yukata* to attend these festivals known as *matsuri*. Everyone dresses up in their best kimonos to attend the *matsuri* – to watch singing and dancing, to play fairground attractions such as the coconut shy and goldfish-catching, and to eat. There'll be stall after stall of wonderful food such as hot dogs, shaved ice with syrups, octopus doughnuts, chocolate-dipped bananas and *Yakisoba* noodles. In one of my favourite Japanese cartoons, *K-On*, a character called Mugi is crestfallen because she goes to a festival and fails to get hold of any *Yakisoba*. She should have made it herself – it's easy enough!

Serves 2 | Takes 15 minutes to make, 12 minutes to cook

300g fresh ramen noodles (*chukamen*) or 125g dried standard thick wheat noodles (*lo mein*) (see Cook's Tip)
1 tbsp groundnut oil
1 small onion, sliced
200g pork belly, thinly sliced, or 2 boneless, skinless chicken thighs, cut into small strips
1 carrot, julienned
1 red pepper, deseeded and sliced
4 Savoy cabbage leaves, sliced
100g beansprouts, topped and tailed
50ml sake or water
salt and pepper to taste

For the sauce
2 tbsp Japanese soy sauce (*shoyu*)
2 tbsp Worcestershire sauce or HP sauce
1 tbsp tomato ketchup
$1/2$ tsp freshly ground black pepper

To garnish
powdered nori seaweed (*aonori*)
red pickled ginger (*kizami shoga*)

If using fresh ramen noodles, loosen and set aside. If using dried noodles, cook according to the packet instructions; drain and rinse with cold water, then set aside.

Combine the sauce ingredients in a small bowl or jug and whisk together.

Heat the oil in a wok or large frying pan on medium heat. Add the onion and stir-fry for 1–2 minutes. Add the meat and stir-fry for 3–4 minutes until it changes colour. Season with a pinch each of salt and pepper and toss the meat to mix.

Now add the carrot, red pepper and cabbage to the wok and stir-fry for another 3–4 minutes. Add the beansprouts and stir-fry for a further minute before adding the noodles. Sprinkle the sake or water over everything and toss over the heat for 1–2 minutes. Finally, add the sauce and mix again to ensure the sauce is distributed evenly.

Divide between 2 pasta dishes. Sprinkle with powdered seaweed and garnish with pickled ginger, then serve immediately, with chopsticks.

Cook's Tip

You may have noticed that despite being called *Yakisoba*, soba noodles are not used to make this dish. Instead, fresh ramen noodles called *chukamen* are traditionally used, although you can substitute wheat noodles as I've suggested or medium egg noodles.

Burmese Stir-fried Noodles

Khao Swè Kyaw (Burma)

Khao Swè Kyaw literally means 'fried noodles', although I like to refer to this as House Special Noodles at my parents' house due to the luxury of the ingredients – three types of meat plus eggs and various vegetables. It's served with salads on the side to cut through any grease or heaviness, as well as a clear broth made from chicken bones, for the same reason. The dish can also be made with mung-bean thread noodles, when it's called *Kyar-zun Kyaw* ('fried vermicelli') – we Burmese are generally laconic when naming our food, though we can be given to flights of fancy.

Serves 4–6 | Takes 35 minutes to make, 30 minutes to cook

300g dried standard thick wheat noodles (*lo mein*)

For the stir-fry
50g pork liver
6 tbsp groundnut oil
1cm piece of fresh root ginger, peeled and finely chopped
2 cloves garlic, finely chopped
100g pork fillet (tenderloin), cut into small strips
3 eggs, beaten and seasoned with salt and pepper
1 tbsp dark soy sauce
1 tbsp caster sugar
50g cauliflower florets
1 large carrot, julienned
1 tennis-ball-sized kohlrabi, peeled and julienned
50g green beans, sliced lengthways

2 tbsp light soy sauce
50g beansprouts, topped and tailed
100g Chinese leaf, sliced
3 spring onions (white part only; keep the green part for the garnish), cut into 2.5cm pieces

For the broth
1 chicken quarter, skinned but still on the bone
$\frac{1}{4}$ tsp MSG or 1 tbsp Marigold bouillon powder
1 tsp salt
1 tsp freshly ground black pepper

To serve
3 spring onions (green part only), shredded
Onion and Tomato Salad (Secret Weapons, page 12)
Cabbage and Cucumber Salad (Secret Weapons, page 11)

Cook the noodles according to the packet instructions. Drain in a colander and rinse thoroughly with running cold water to prevent further cooking. Set to one side in the colander so that any residual water can continue to drain.

Chill the pork liver in the freezer for 30 minutes (to make slicing easier), then cut it into small strips.

While the liver is freezing, put the ingredients for the broth in a saucepan, add 500ml water and bring to the boil. Reduce the heat to medium-low and simmer for 20 minutes. Remove the chicken, strip the meat and set to one side. Put the bones back into the broth and keep it simmering gently.

Heat 2 tablespoons oil in a wok or deep frying pan. When it starts to sizzle, turn the heat down to medium and add the ginger and garlic. Stir-fry for 1–2 minutes until fragrant. Add the pork and fry for 1–2 minutes until cooked through. Empty the contents of the wok into a dish and set to one side.

Add another 2 tablespoons oil to the wok and heat on a medium heat. Add the beaten egg and move the pan around to spread the egg out evenly into a thin omelette. When the omelette is firm all the way through and golden on the base, use a spatula to ease around its edges and flip the omelette over. Cook for a further 1–2 minutes until golden on both sides. Tip the omelette on to a plate, cut into strips and set to one side.

Heat the remaining 2 tablespoons oil in the wok on a high heat, then tip in the pork and chicken strips. Sprinkle with the dark soy and sugar and mix thoroughly. Add the cauliflower, carrot, kohlrabi and green beans. Stir-fry for 2–3 minutes, then add the pork liver and stir-fry for a minute until the liver turns opaque.

Now add the noodles, light soy and 100ml water. Mix thoroughly to combine and stir-fry for 1–2 minutes. Add the beansprouts, Chinese leaf, spring onions and omelette strips. Mix once more and stir-fry gently for 2–3 minutes, then divide among 4 pasta dishes.

Pour the chicken broth into 4 small soup bowls and add the spring onion greens and black pepper. Serve the noodles with chopsticks or spoons and forks, with the bowls of soup and the salads on the side.

Stir-fried Sweet-potato Noodles

Japchae (Korea)

Japchae (aka *Jabchae* or *Chapchae*) is a Korean dish made from sweet-potato noodles, which are rarely used in other countries. It's usually a side dish, often with *Bulgogi*, a Korean beef dish, and is even sometimes part of a double-carb combo on a bed of rice, when it's known as *Japchae-bap*. Traditionally served at parties and other special occasions in Korea, the dish is also great for picnics, since it can be served cold or at room temperature as well as hot. I think it's best at room temperature.

Serves 2 | Takes 20 minutes to make, 8 minutes to cook

150g lean boneless beef, such as frying steak or flank steak, cut into thin strips
small handful of dried wood-ear mushrooms
200g dried sweet-potato noodles (*dangmyeon*)
2 tbsp groundnut oil
1 large carrot, julienned
1 medium onion, thinly sliced
6 fresh shiitake mushrooms, sliced
6 spring onions (green and white parts), cut into 2.5cm lengths
large handful of baby spinach leaves, washed
1 tbsp sesame seeds

For the beef marinade
4 cloves garlic, finely chopped
2 tsp golden caster sugar
2 tbsp light soy sauce
1 tbsp toasted sesame oil
1 tsp Chinese rice wine or dry sherry

For the dressing
4 tbsp dark soy sauce
2 tbsp golden caster sugar
3 tbsp toasted sesame oil

Combine the beef with its marinade ingredients in a bowl and leave to marinate for 15 minutes.

Put the wood-ear mushrooms in a heatproof bowl, generously cover with just-boiled water and leave to soak for 15 minutes until soft. Drain and slice, then set to one side.

While the mushrooms are soaking, cook the noodles according to the packet instructions (try not to overcook them – they should be soft but chewy); drain and rinse immediately in running cold water. If you like, snip the noodles with scissors into shorter lengths to make them easier to eat. Set to one side.

Whisk the dressing ingredients together and set to one side.

Heat the groundnut oil in a wok or large frying pan on medium-high heat. Add the marinated beef and stir-fry for 3–4 minutes until the beef is cooked. Add the carrot, onion and shiitake and wood-ear mushrooms, and stir-fry for another 3–4 minutes until the onion is translucent. Add the spring onions and stir-fry for a further minute before removing from the heat.

Put the noodles, beef and vegetable mix, spinach and dressing in a large serving bowl or dish and mix thoroughly to combine. Sprinkle with the sesame seeds and serve warm or at room temperature. Give people bowls and chopsticks and tell them to tuck in.

Stir-fried Noodles with Omelette

Khua Mee/Kuy Teav Cha (Laos/Cambodia)

Also called *Khaw Mee*, this is a simple dish from Laos, similar enough to *Kuy Teav Cha* from Cambodia to be classed together. Caramelised rice noodles are topped with omelette strips to make a unusual but satisfying dish.

Serves 4 | Takes 15 minutes to make, 15 minutes to cook

- **400g dried narrow, flat rice noodles (*bánh pho*, if possible)**
- **100g beansprouts, topped and tailed**
- **6 tbsp groundnut oil**
- **50g palm sugar or soft dark brown sugar**
- **4 cloves garlic, sliced**
- **1 medium onion, sliced**
- **100g cooked, peeled tiger prawns**

For the omelette strips
- **4 eggs**
- **1 tsp golden caster sugar**
- **1 tsp light soy sauce**
- **1 tsp fish sauce**

For the sauce
- **2 tbsp fish sauce**
- **3 tbsp dark soy sauce**
- **2 tbsp oyster sauce**

To garnish
- **juice of 1/2 lime**
- **1 tbsp salted peanuts, crushed**
- **handful of fresh coriander leaves, chopped**
- **6 spring onions (green and white parts), thinly sliced**

Put the rice noodles into a heatproof bowl, generously cover with just-boiled water and leave to soak for 15 minutes. Drain, untangle and set to one side. While you're soaking the noodles, blanch the beansprouts by pouring just-boiled water over them and draining straight away.

Now make the omelette strips. Whisk the eggs with the rest of the omelette ingredients plus 2 tablespoons water. Heat 1 tablespoon oil in a frying pan on a medium-high heat and pour in enough egg mix to form a thin layer, like a crêpe. Cook for a minute, then flip or turn over and cook for another minute. Slide the omelette on to a chopping board, and make the next omelette. Repeat the process until you have used up all the egg mix. Roll up the omelettes and cut across into thin strips. Set to one side.

For the caramelised noodles, add the remaining 4 tablespoons oil and the palm sugar to a wok or large frying pan and heat on a medium-high heat for 4–5 minutes until the sugar has dissolved and starts to caramelise. Swirl the syrup in the wok a few times so it browns evenly, then add the garlic and onion and stir-fry in the caramel sauce for 4–5 minutes until fragrant.

Now add the sauce ingredients with 50ml water and stir vigorously to combine. Turn the heat up to high and fry for 2–3 minutes.

Add the noodles and toss gently to ensure they are evenly covered in sauce. Add the beansprouts and toss again to mix before dishing up on a serving platter. Squeeze the lime juice over the noodles, then top with the prawns and omelette strips.

Scatter the crushed peanuts on top and sprinkle with the coriander and spring onions. Give everyone noodle bowls and chopsticks and let them help themselves.

Cook's Tip
This can be made vegetarian very easily by replacing the prawns with fried tofu, substituting Indonesian sweet soy sauce (*kecap manis*) for oyster sauce, and using liquid aminos or Maggi seasoning instead of fish sauce.

Drunken Noodles

Pad Kee Mao (Laos/Thailand)

This is a distinctive dish due to its use of holy basil – a spicy liquorice-like herb with no real substitute. *Pad Kee Mao*, or *Pad Ki Mao*, arrived in Laos and Thailand via Chinese traders and has been wholeheartedly adopted by both countries. As for its name, there are various theories. It is considered a great cure for a hangover, so perhaps it should be called 'Drunkards' Noodles' instead. It's also speculated – mainly by Westerners – that it is so spicy that it can only be eaten with whisky and beer to drown it out, or that you'd have to be drunk to take the heat. I've been quite moderate with the chilli quantities below, but feel free to add more!

Serves 4 | Takes 15 minutes to make, 10 minutes to cook

400g dried broad, flat rice noodles (*ho fun*)
3 tbsp groundnut oil
1 medium onion, sliced
4 cloves garlic, finely chopped
2 boneless, skinless chicken thighs, about 250g total weight, cut into strips
2 fresh, red bird's eye chillies, smashed
1 tbsp palm sugar or soft dark brown sugar
1 green pepper, deseeded and sliced
8 baby corn
3 eggs, beaten
1 fresh red finger chilli, sliced
large handful of fresh holy basil leaves (or Thai basil, if necessary)

For the sauce
2 tbsp oyster sauce
2 tbsp sweet soy sauce
1 tbsp light soy sauce
1 tbsp rice vinegar
1 tbsp fish sauce
juice of 1/4 lime

To serve
1 bulb of Pickled Garlic (Secret Weapons, page 12), thinly sliced
6 spring onions (white part only), julienned
handful of fresh coriander leaves, chopped
handful of salted peanuts, crushed

Put the noodles in a large heatproof bowl and generously cover with just-boiled water. After a minute, untangle the noodles, then leave them to soak for a further 6 minutes until al dente. Drain in a colander and rinse thoroughly under running cold water. Set to one side in the colander so that any residual water can continue to drain.

While the noodles are soaking, combine the ingredients for the sauce in a jug and whisk to mix. Set aside.

Heat 2 tablespoons oil in a wok or large frying pan on medium-high heat. Add the onion and garlic and stir-fry for 2 minutes until fragrant. Add the chicken, bird's eye chillies and sugar and stir-fry for 3 minutes until the chicken is no longer pink.

Add the green pepper and baby corn and stir-fry for another 3–4 minutes. Now push everything to the side of the wok and add the remaining tablespoon of oil to the cleared space. Pour the eggs into the oil and scramble them. Push the eggs to the side and pour the whisked sauce into the cleared space. Once the sauce is simmering, add the noodles and toss gently to mix all the ingredients together and ensure even distribution of the sauce.

Remove from the heat. Add the finger chilli and the holy basil leaves and toss to combine and wilt the basil. Dish up on a serving platter and garnish with the pickled garlic, spring onions, coriander and peanuts. Give everyone a plate, spoon and fork, and tell them to help themselves.

Tofu, Chinese Broccoli and Black Bean Noodles

(fusion)

Sometimes you need a dish that makes you feel saintly. This is that dish – light but spicy and delicious, vegan without the hair shirt....

Serves 2 | Takes 12 minutes to make, 12 minutes to cook

125g dried standard thick wheat noodles (*lo mein*)
1 tbsp Indonesian sweet soy sauce (*kecap manis*)
1 tbsp dark soy sauce
1 tbsp light soy sauce
1 tsp golden caster sugar
50ml vegetable stock
2 tbsp groundnut oil
6 cloves garlic, finely sliced
1cm piece of fresh root ginger, peeled and julienned
1 tsp fermented black beans, finely chopped
100g Chinese broccoli (*kai-lan*)
150g extra-firm tofu, cut into 2.5cm cubes
1 tsp toasted sesame oil

Cook the noodles according to the packet instructions. Drain in a colander and rinse thoroughly with running cold water to prevent further cooking. Set to one side in the colander so that any residual water continues to drain.

Whisk together the 3 soy sauces, sugar and vegetable stock in a small bowl. Set aside.

Heat the groundnut oil in a wok or deep frying pan. When it starts to sizzle, turn the heat down to medium and add the garlic and ginger. Stir-fry for 1–2 minutes until fragrant, then add the black beans and stir-fry for another minute.

Now add the broccoli and stir-fry for a minute before adding the tofu and the soy sauce mix. Toss gently to combine, then stir-fry for a further 2–3 minutes.

Add the noodles and fry, tossing and stirring gently, for another 2–3 minutes. Try not to break up the tofu too much. Divide between 2 pasta dishes, drizzle the sesame oil over the top and serve, with spoons and forks.

Braised Soy Mushrooms with Chives and E-fu Noodles (fusion)

In the same way you might consider tuna and monkfish to be the 'meatiest' members of the fish world, shiitake and eringi mushrooms are the 'meat' of the fungus world – by which I mean they can take centre stage in many dishes – and go well with strong flavours such as the garlic chives used here, which are huge, flat-bladed and garlicky, quite different from the chives you might have growing in your garden. The noodles in this dish are equally robust, so it's a surprisingly hearty – and quick – meal.

Serves 2 | Takes 10 minutes to make, 10 minutes to cook

200g dried thick egg noodles
   (e-fu)
2 tbsp groundnut oil
100g shiitake mushrooms,
   sliced
100g eringi mushrooms or
   chestnut mushrooms, sliced
3 tbsp dark soy sauce
2 tbsp light soy sauce
1 tbsp chilli bean sauce
1 tbsp toasted sesame oil
4 garlic chives, finely chopped

Prepare the noodles according to the packet instructions; drain and set to one side.

Heat the groundnut oil in a wok or deep frying pan on a high heat. When the oil starts to sizzle, add all the mushrooms and stir-fry for 2–3 minutes until they wilt slightly. Add the soy sauces, the chilli bean sauce and 2 tablespoons cold water, and stir-fry for another 2–3 minutes.

With the heat still on high, add the noodles and the toasted sesame oil, mix thoroughly and stir-fry for 2–3 more minutes.

Sprinkle on the chives and stir to combine, then dish up into 2 pasta dishes. Serve with chopsticks or forks and spoons.

Teriyaki Salmon Noodles
(fusion)

Teriyaki is a Japanese cooking technique where food is grilled while being basted with a sweet and salty marinade – 'teri' refers to the shine given by the sugar in the marinade, and 'yaki' refers to grilling. This dish is far from authentic Japanese cuisine however, as here the salmon is baked rather than grilled, and the recipe owes more to the United States with its use of pak choi and egg noodles, which is why I've proudly called it fusion.

Serves 2 | Takes 15 minutes to make, 15 minutes to cook

2 pieces of salmon fillet (skin on), about 150g each
200g fresh or dried egg noodles (available from any supermarket)
1 tbsp groundnut oil
1 tsp toasted sesame oil
2 baby pak choi, chopped
1 tbsp sesame seeds, toasted
2 spring onions (green and white parts), finely chopped
lime wedges, to serve

For the teriyaki sauce
4 tbsp dark soy sauce
2 tbsp mirin
2 tbsp sake
1 tbsp palm sugar or soft dark brown sugar
2cm knob of fresh root ginger, peeled and grated

Preheat the oven to 220°C/Gas Mark 7. First make the teriyaki sauce. Combine all the ingredients in a small saucepan and cook on a medium heat for 5 minutes until thickened. Leave to cool slightly.

Brush the sauce all over the salmon and place it, skin side up, in a foil-lined baking tin. Leave to marinate for 5 minutes, then bake for 10 minutes.

Meanwhile, cook the noodles according to the packet instructions; drain. Heat the groundnut and sesame oils together in a wok or large frying pan on a medium heat, add the pak choi and sesame seeds, and stir-fry for a couple of minutes. Add the noodles and the spring onions, and stir and toss to mix thoroughly.

Divide the noodles between 2 pasta dishes and top each with a salmon fillet. Serve with lime wedges, and spoons and forks.

SOUPS

Roast Duck Noodle Soup

(China/Hong Kong)

Originally from Hong Kong, this soup is a Chinatown favourite all over the world. Every restaurant has its own version, but it's so easy to make at home, especially if you cheat and buy a portion of those beautiful lacquered Chinese roast ducks you see swinging in the window of your favourite takeaway.

Serves 2 | Takes 15 minutes to make, 25 minutes to cook

125g dried standard thick wheat noodles (*lo mein*)
1 litre chicken stock
1 tbsp Chinese rice wine or dry sherry
1cm piece of fresh root ginger, peeled and sliced
1 tsp five spice powder
1/2 Chinese roast duck, boned and chopped into bite-sized pieces (see Cook's Tip)
300g choy sum, sliced
2 spring onions (green and white parts), thinly sliced
2 tsp toasted sesame oil

Cook the noodles according to the packet instructions. Drain in a colander and rinse thoroughly with running cold water to prevent further cooking. Set to one side in the colander so that any residual water continues to drain.

Pour the chicken stock into a medium saucepan and bring to the boil. Add the rice wine, ginger and five spice. Turn the heat down to medium-low, cover with a lid and leave to simmer gently for 20 minutes.

Just before the end of the simmering time, reheat the noodles by placing the colander in the sink and pouring a kettle of boiling water over them. Shake the colander to drain the noodles, then divide them between 2 noodle bowls.

Add the duck pieces and choy sum to the simmering stock and heat for 2–3 minutes – just enough time to warm the duck and wilt the choy sum – then ladle over the noodles. Top with the spring onions and drizzle over the sesame oil. Serve immediately, with chopsticks and Chinese spoons.

Cook's Tip

I love to roast whole duck at home, but it's time-consuming, so I often just roast 2 duck legs: sprinkle them with salt and brush with 1 tablespoon each honey and soy sauce, then roast at 180°C/Gas Mark 4 for 45 minutes. I'm also more than happy to buy a portion of Chinese roast duck from a takeaway.

Fish Ball Noodle Soup

(China/Hong Kong/Singapore)

If you've never had a fish ball before, let me explain. These delectable Asian morsels are made from white fish that is pounded, rather than ground, giving a light, smooth and bouncy texture to the balls. Because of this, fish balls bob pleasingly in soup.

Serves 2 | Takes 20 minutes to make, 20 minutes to cook

200g dried rice vermicelli noodles
75g dried anchovies (*ikan bilis*)
1cm piece of fresh root ginger, peeled and sliced
2 cloves garlic, sliced
1 tbsp light soy sauce
1 tsp caster sugar
200g ready-made fish balls, halved

To serve
Lard Pieces in Lard Oil (Secret Weapons, page 12)
4 cos or iceberg lettuce leaves, thinly sliced
2 spring onions (green and white parts), finely chopped
Fried Shallots (see Secret Weapons, page 11)
Chilli Soy Dip (Secret Weapons, page 11)

Put the noodles into a heatproof bowl. Pour over plenty of just-boiled water and untangle the noodles with a fork, then leave to soak for 15 minutes. Drain in a colander and rinse with running cold water. Set to one side in the colander so they can continue to drain.

Discard the heads from the anchovies (just break them off), then soak the anchovies in warm water for 5 minutes; drain and rinse well with cold water. Put the anchovies in a medium saucepan with 1 litre water, add the ginger and garlic and bring to the boil. Reduce the heat to medium-low and simmer for 15 minutes. Scoop out the anchovies with a slotted spoon and discard (otherwise they will make the broth bitter).

Add the soy sauce and sugar to the broth and bring back to a simmer before adding the fish balls. Simmer for a few minutes – when they're cooked, they will float to the top.

Now divide the noodles between 2 bowls. Ladle the fish balls and broth over them, then drizzle on the lard pieces and lard oil. Garnish with the lettuce, spring onions and fried shallots. Serve each bowl with chopsticks and a Chinese spoon, with a saucer of chilli soy dip alongside.

Crossing-the-bridge Noodles

Guòqiáo Mǐxiàn (China)

This is one of the best-known dishes from the Yunnan region in China. The traditional tale behind its name tells of a scholar who secluded himself on a small island to study for his imperial exams. His wife would bring him noodle soup to sustain him, but found that by the time she had crossed the bridge to the island, the soup would be cold and the noodles soggy. So she decided to ladle the broth into an earthenware pot, with a layer of oil on top to keep the broth warm, and to carry the noodles and other ingredients in a separate container. Only when she was ready to serve, did she mix everything together to give her husband a wonderfully warming meal.

Serves 4 | Takes 30 minutes to make, 2 hours to cook

300g dried thick, round rice noodles (Vietnamese *bún* or Guilin rice vermicelli)
1 sheet of beancurd skin
6 dried shiitake mushrooms
small handful of dried wood-ear mushrooms
100g skinless, boneless chicken breast fillet, sliced paper-thin
100g pork fillet (tenderloin), sliced paper-thin
12 raw king prawns, peeled, deveined and butterflied
50g slices of prosciutto (Parma ham) or jamon (Serrano or Ibérico)
1 small pak choi, leaves separated, or handful of baby spinach leaves
4 tbsp preserved mustard greens, chopped
6 garlic chives, cut into 2.5cm lengths

For the broth

1 chicken carcass
4 chicken wings
2 cloves garlic, peeled
1cm piece of fresh root ginger, peeled and sliced
6 spring onions (white part only; keep the green part for the garnish), sliced
1 tbsp Chinese rice wine or dry sherry
1 tbsp caster sugar
1 tbsp light soy sauce
1 tsp salt

To garnish

4 quail's eggs
6 spring onions (green part only), sliced
handful of fresh coriander leaves, chopped
Fresh Chilli Garlic Sauce (Secret Weapons, page 11)

To make the broth, put the chicken carcass and wings, garlic, ginger, spring onions, rice wine and sugar in a large saucepan and add 2 litres water. Bring to the boil, then turn the heat down to low and simmer for 2 hours, skimming off any scum from the surface from time to time.

Strain the broth into a clean pan. Pick the meat from the carcass and wings and set to one side; discard the rest of the solids (including the chicken skin). Add the soy sauce and salt to the broth and set the saucepan to one side.

Put the rice noodles in a large heatproof bowl and generously cover with just-boiled water. Leave to soak for 1 hour. Drain in a colander and rinse thoroughly with running cold water, then set to one side in the colander so that any residual water can continue to drain.

Place the beancurd skin in a large heatproof dish or baking tray, generously cover with just-boiled water and leave to soak for 15 minutes until soft. Drain and cut into 2.5cm pieces, then set aside.

Put the shiitake and wood-ear mushrooms in a heatproof bowl, generously cover with just-boiled water and leave to soak for 15 minutes until soft. Drain (reserving the soaking liquid) and slice the mushrooms. Set aside. Add the mushroom soaking liquid to the saucepan of broth.

Place a portion of chicken breast, pork, prawns, prosciutto, beancurd skin, pak choi, mustard greens, garlic chives and rice noodles in each of 4 noodle bowls.

Bring the saucepan of broth back to the boil, then ladle it into each bowl – the steaming broth will lightly cook all the ingredients. Crack a quail's egg into each bowl and garnish with spring onions and coriander. Serve with chopsticks and Chinese spoons, with chilli garlic sauce on the side.

Hand-Torn Noodles

Ban Mian/Pan Mee (China/Malaysia)

This is a Hakka Chinese dish notable for its pleasingly clumsy noodles, which you make by tearing off bits of dough and boiling in stock. Although the dish can be served in various ways, it normally comes in an anchovy soup, and is served with a leafy vegetable and more anchovies on top.

Serves 4 | Takes 1 hour 30 minutes to make, 1 hour 30 minutes to cook

6 dried shiitake mushrooms
small handful of dried wood-ear mushrooms
250g minced pork
4 cloves garlic, finely chopped
1 medium onion, finely chopped

For the noodle dough
300g plain flour
$\frac{1}{2}$ tsp salt
1 egg
1 tsp toasted sesame oil

For the pork marinade
1 tsp Chinese rice wine or dry sherry
1 tsp oyster sauce
1 tsp light soy sauce
1 tsp dark soy sauce
1 tsp cornflour
$\frac{1}{2}$ tsp caster sugar
$\frac{1}{2}$ tsp toasted sesame oil
salt and white pepper to taste

For the broth
4 tbsp groundnut oil
400g dried anchovies (*ikan bilis*), heads removed, rinsed well

1 medium onion, quartered
2cm knob of fresh root ginger, peeled and smashed
4 garlic cloves, peeled
$\frac{1}{4}$ tsp MSG or 1 tbsp Marigold bouillon powder
1 tbsp fish sauce
1 tsp caster sugar
1 tsp salt

To garnish
100g choy sum (see Cook's Tip)
Fried Shallots (Secret Weapons, page 11)
Crispy Garlic Oil (Secret Weapons, page 11)
4 spring onions (green and white parts), julienned
Chilli Soy Dip (Secret Weapons, page 11)

First make the noodle dough. Sift the flour and salt into a mixing bowl and make a well in the centre. Crack the egg into the well and break its yolk, then add 3 tablespoons cold water and the sesame oil. Using chopsticks, stir everything together gently until slowly but surely a dough forms. Turn out on to a work surface dusted with a little flour and knead the dough until smooth. Put the dough back in the mixing bowl, cover with clingfilm and chill for 1 hour.

Meanwhile, put the shiitake and wood-ear mushrooms in a heatproof bowl, generously cover with just-boiled water and leave to soak for 15 minutes until soft. Drain (reserving the soaking liquid) and slice the mushrooms. Set aside.

Combine the mince with its marinade ingredients and leave to marinate while you make the broth.

Heat the oil in a wok or large frying pan on a medium-high heat. Add the anchovies and stir-fry for 2–3 minutes until crisp and fragrant. Remove with a slotted spoon and drain on kitchen paper (reserve the oil in the wok). Set half the anchovies aside for the garnish – they should crisp up as they cool.

Put the remaining anchovies in a stockpot or large saucepan with the rest of the broth ingredients and add 2 litres water and the mushroom soaking liquid. Bring to the boil, then turn down the heat and simmer for 1 hour. Strain into a clean pan and discard all the solids. Set the broth aside.

While the broth is simmering, blanch the choy sum by pouring just-boiled water over them and draining straight away. Set to one side.

Reheat the oil in the wok and add the garlic and onion. Stir-fry for 3–4 minutes until fragrant. Add the marinated pork and stir-fry for 5–6 minutes until the pork is cooked, breaking it up as you go. Add 50ml water to moisten and stir-fry for a further 2–3 minutes. Set to one side.

Now make your noodles. Bring the broth back to a rolling boil over a high heat. Divide the dough into quarters. Dust your hands with flour, then take one portion of dough and pinch some of it out to flatten it to about 3mm thick. Tear off a piece of the flattened dough (about the size of a 50p coin) and drop it into the bubbling stock. Repeat until you've used all the dough in that portion – you will need to work quickly so you don't overcook the first noodles you make. The noodles are cooked when they float to the surface. Scoop them out with a slotted spoon and transfer to a noodle bowl. Repeat the process with the remaining 3 portions of dough.

Top the noodles in the 4 bowls with the fried minced pork, sliced mushrooms and blanched choy sum. Bring the broth back to the boil, then ladle it over the noodles, reheating everything in the process. Top with the reserved fried anchovies, fried shallots, garlic oil and spring onions. Serve immediately, with chopsticks and Chinese spoons, and chilli soy dip on the side.

Cook's Tip

This really ought to be served with katuk leaf, whose Latin name is *Sauropus androgynus* (known in Malaysia as *sayur manis*). I'm fairly certain we can't get this vegetable in the UK, but choy sum is a good substitute, as is pak choi.

Wonton Noodle Soup

Wonton Mein (China/Hong Kong)

A Cantonese classic, this is popular in China, Hong Kong, Malaysia, Singapore and Thailand. In Hong Kong, the wontons are usually filled with prawns, but I prefer a mix of prawn and pork. Other versions are topped with slices of Chinese barbecue pork (*char siu*). My parents tell me that when they first arrived in the UK, they could get tins of wonton soup, which were amazing – all you had to do was heat the contents of the tin and pour them on top of cooked noodles. Sadly, I never got to partake of these legendary tins, so I comfort myself by making wonton noodle soup from scratch instead. It's a tad fiddly, but completely worth it and looks very impressive.

Serves 4 | Takes 45 minutes to make, 30 minutes to cook

20 wonton wrappers
1 egg, beaten with 1 tbsp cold water, for the egg wash
300g dried thin egg noodles (*you mian*)
4 baby pak choi

For the wonton filling
200g minced pork
200g raw prawns, peeled, deveined and finely chopped
6 garlic chives, thinly sliced
1cm piece of fresh root ginger, peeled and finely chopped
1 tsp cornflour
1 tbsp Chinese rice wine or dry sherry
2 tbsp light soy sauce
2 tbsp toasted sesame oil
1 tbsp cracked white peppercorns

For the wonton soup
1 tbsp groundnut oil
handful of dried shrimps
1.5 litres chicken stock
1cm piece of fresh root ginger, peeled and sliced

To serve
6 spring onions, thinly sliced
4 tsp toasted sesame oil
Fresh Chilli Garlic Sauce (Secret Weapons, page 11)

Combine the wonton filling ingredients in a large bowl and mix well. To make each wonton, put a level teaspoonful of filling in the middle of a wonton wrapper. Brush the edges with egg wash. Fold the wrapper over to form a triangle and seal the edges together by pressing down. Brush egg wash on one corner of the triangle and fold again gently so this egg-washed corner meets another corner. Press these 2 corners together so they stick. As they are made, place the wontons on a tray or large plate, in one layer and spaced apart so they don't stick together. Cover loosely with a damp cloth or clingfilm to prevent them from drying out.

Cook the noodles according to the packet instructions; drain and set to one side. Blanch the pak choi by pouring just-boiled water over them and then draining straight away. Divide the noodles and pak choi among 4 noodle bowls.

Now make the soup. Heat the oil in a stockpot or large saucepan on a high heat. Add the dried shrimps and stir-fry for 1–2 minutes until fragrant. Add the chicken stock and ginger slices and bring to the boil.

Add a quarter of the wontons and wait for them to float to the top – this shows that they're cooked. Scoop out the wontons with a slotted spoon and place in one of the noodle bowls. Bring the soup back to the boil and repeat the process for the other portions.

Bring the soup back to the boil one last time, then ladle into the bowls, which will reheat the noodles, wontons and pak choi. Garnish with spring onions and drizzle over the sesame oil. Serve immediately, with chopsticks and Chinese spoons, and chilli garlic sauce on the side.

Miso Ramen

(Japan)

Miso Ramen is also known as Sapporo Ramen, because it comes from Sapporo in Hokkaido, the northern-most region of Japan. It's one of the simpler ramen dishes to make, but its use of butter and sweetcorn as toppings gives it a marvellous taste and texture.

Serves 4 | Takes 20 minutes to make, 3 hours to cook

400g fresh ramen noodles (*chūkamen*)

For the broth

2 litres chicken, pork or vegetable stock
2cm knob of fresh root ginger, peeled and smashed
1 whole leek, trimmed
1 tbsp caster sugar
1 tbsp sake
1 tbsp mirin
1 tbsp instant dashi granules
2 tbsp white miso paste (*shiro miso*)
2 tbsp red miso paste (*aka miso*)
2 tbsp hot water

For the toppings

12 slices of Braised Pork Belly (Secret Weapons, page 10)
4 heaped tbsp unsalted butter
100g beansprouts, topped and tailed
100g tinned sweetcorn, drained
2 Ramen Eggs (Secret Weapons, page 12) or soft-boiled eggs
2 spring onions (green and white parts), shredded
Japanese pickled bamboo shoots (*menma*)
shichimi pepper (*shichimi togarashi*)

Put the stock, ginger and leek in a stockpot or large saucepan and bring to the boil. Turn the heat down to medium-low. Add the sugar, sake, mirin and instant dashi and stir to mix, then leave the broth to simmer for 30 minutes. Discard the ginger and leek.

Mix the 2 types of miso with the hot water in a bowl, then add to the broth. Add the ramen noodles and pork slices and simmer for 3 minutes.

Ladle the broth and noodles into 4 ramen bowls and add a rounded spoonful of butter to each. Garnish each bowl with 3 fanned-out slices of pork, some beansprouts, sweetcorn, half an egg, spring onions, bamboo shoots and shichimi pepper to taste. Serve with chopsticks and ramen ladles.

Pork Bone Ramen

Tonkotsu Ramen (Japan)

Ramen noodles originally came to Japan from China (it's thought that the name came from '*la mian*', which is a type of Chinese noodle), but by the 1950s they were firmly embraced by the Japanese. These days, it's not uncommon to see famous ramen chefs from around Japan come together for ramen festivals and cook-offs, to see who makes the mightiest regional ramen dish. *Tonkotsu Ramen* comes from the Kyushu region of Japan, and is legendary for the time it takes to get it just right. Its broth is cloudy, which is unusual, but this is because of all the porky goodness infused into it (*tonkotsu* means 'pork bones'). Once you've made the broth, though, you can store it, and when it comes to eating, you can add whatever note you like to the base – for example, sweet and salty with miso, fiery with chilli bean sauce, or soothing with sesame paste.

Serves 6–8 | Takes 30 minutes to make, 8 hours to cook

400g fresh ramen noodles (*chūkamen*)

For the broth
6 tbsp groundnut oil
1 medium onion, quartered
1 garlic bulb, ends sliced off (skin still on)
3cm knob of fresh root ginger, smashed (skin still on)
2 pig's trotters, cut in half lengthways
2kg pork bones, cracked and chopped into pieces
2 raw chicken carcasses
500g piece of pork back fat
6 spring onions (white parts only; save the green parts for the garnish), tied in a bundle with string

To season (choose one of the following)
salt
Japanese soy sauce (*shoyu*)
finely chopped garlic
Chinese sesame paste or tahini
chilli bean sauce

To serve
Braised Pork Belly (Secret Weapons page 10)
3–4 Ramen Eggs (Secret Weapons, page 12) or soft-boiled eggs
6 spring onions (green parts only), thinly sliced
Black Garlic Oil (Secret Weapons, page 10)
dried nori seaweed, cut into squares
shichimi pepper (*shichimi togarashi*)

First make the broth. Heat the oil in a non-stick or cast-iron wok or frying pan on a medium-high heat. Add the onion, garlic and ginger and stir-fry for 10–15 minutes until they're so caramelised that they're almost black. Remove to a plate and set to one side.

Combine the trotters, pork bones and chicken carcasses in a large stockpot and cover with cold water. Bring to the boil, then drain. Rinse and rub the bones thoroughly under cold running water, removing any dark bits (blood and marrow) that you can see.

Transfer the bones to a clean stockpot and add the caramelised vegetables, pork fat and the spring onion white parts. Pour in enough cold water to cover the ingredients by 2cm. Bring to a rolling boil, skimming off any impurities that rise. Keep boiling and skimming for 20–25 minutes until no more scum forms, then cover the stockpot with a heavy lid to prevent it from boiling over and reduce the heat slightly. Keep it on a slow rolling boil for 7–8 hours until the broth is cloudy and as thick as single cream. You will need to be on standby to top up the water from time to time, in order to keep the bones submerged. If you have to go out, turn the heat down to its lowest setting; then, when you come back, bring it back to the boil and continue as before.

At the end of the broth simmering time, strain it twice through a sieve lined with muslin; discard all the solids. You can now freeze the broth for up to a month, refrigerate overnight or serve it straight away.

For each serving, pour 500ml of the broth into a small saucepan and add 1 teaspoon of any one of the seasonings. Heat on a medium-high heat, then add a portion of ramen noodles and pork belly slices and simmer for 3 minutes.

Ladle the broth and noodles into a ramen bowl, and garnish with fanned-out slices of pork, half a ramen egg, some spring onion greens, black garlic oil, seaweed and shichimi pepper to taste. Serve with chopsticks and ramen ladles.

Iron Pot Udon

Nabeyaki Udon (Japan)

If you're feeling in need of warmth and comfort, this Japanese dish will drive the chill away. Traditionally cooked and served in a *nabe* – a pot made of clay or cast iron – its ingredients vary, so feel free to use whatever you have to hand. It's almost always topped with tempura, which is worth any extra effort.

Serves 2 | Takes 30 minutes to make, 30 minutes to cook

200g dried udon noodles or 300g fresh (*yude udon*)
1 skinless, boneless chicken thigh, about 150g, cut into bite-size pieces
75ml each of mirin and sake
1 tbsp caster sugar
50ml light soy sauce
750ml Dashi (page 9)
4 slices of any Japanese fishcake (*kamaboko, naruto or chikuwa*)
1/2 tsp salt

For the tempura prawns and squash

1/2 small Japanese squash (kabocha) or harlequin squash
6 very large, raw prawns (king or tiger), peeled and deveined
120g plain flour
1/2 tsp bicarbonate of soda
1 egg, chilled
250ml iced water
groundnut oil for deep-frying

To serve
handful of fresh baby spinach leaves

2 eggs
2 spring onions (green and white parts), sliced on the diagonal into 3cm sections
handful of dried nori seaweed strips
shichimi pepper (*shichimi togarashi*)

If using dried *udon*, bring a medium saucepan half full of water to the boil. Scatter the noodles into the water, then immediately reduce the heat to medium-low and simmer for 15 minutes. Drain the noodles in a colander set in the sink. Run cold water over them while you rub and swish them with your hand to rinse them. If using fresh *udon*, blanch them by pouring just-boiled water over them in a bowl and leaving them for 5 minutes. Drain and set to one side.

Put the chicken, mirin, sake, sugar and 100ml water in a small saucepan and bring to the boil, stirring so the sugar dissolves. Simmer for 5 minutes until the chicken is poached, then remove from heat and stir in the soy sauce. Leave to cool.

To prepare the tempura ingredients, cut the squash into thin wedges (skin on), discarding the seeds. Cut notches along the sides of each prawn, then bend it against its natural curve so it straightens out. Set to one side.

Next make the broth. Slowly bring the dashi just up to the boil in a medium saucepan. Stir in the chicken and soy sauce mixture, the fishcake and salt. Remove from the heat and keep warm.

Now make the tempura batter. Sift the flour and bicarbonate of soda into a bowl and make a well in the centre. Add the chilled egg and iced water. Using chopsticks, break the egg yolk, then whisk everything together lightly 3 or 4 times (for no more than 5 seconds). The batter is meant to look lumpy.

Heat a wok with a 6cm depth of oil on a medium-high heat until you can feel waves of heat coming off the top of the oil with the palm of your hand. Have a rack ready to drain your tempura.

One by one, dip the pieces of squash in the lumpy batter, then lay gently in the hot oil. Do not crowd the wok. The squash slices should fizz and sizzle gently. Leave for 20 seconds, then turn them over with a slotted spoon or chopsticks and fry for another 20 seconds – they should turn golden brown. Lift out and drain on the rack. Remove any bits of batter in the wok (you can save these to use as garnish) before frying the next batch. When you've fried all the squash, repeat the process with the prawns. Tempura goes soft and soggy very quickly, so you need to finish the dish without delay.

Divide the noodles between 2 noodle bowls and top with the baby spinach. Bring the dashi broth back to the boil, then ladle the chicken, fishcake and broth over the noodles so they are swimming; the spinach will wilt. Quickly slip an egg into each bowl so it can poach very lightly in the hot broth. Garnish with the tempura prawns and squash, spring onions, nori and shichimi pepper to taste. Serve immediately, with chopsticks and Chinese spoons.

Moon-Viewing Udon

Tsukimi Udon (Japan)

Tsukimi **literally means 'moon-viewing' – this is a big event in Japan that happens in mid-autumn. These noodles are therefore eaten to celebrate the event, and the egg that tops the dish is meant to represent the harvest moon.**

Serves 4 | Takes 30 minutes to make, 20 minutes to cook

400g dried udon noodles or 600g fresh (*yude udon*)
150ml mirin
150ml sake
1 tbsp caster sugar
100ml light soy sauce
1.5 litres Dashi (page 9)
4 large eggs, or 4 Hot Spring Eggs (Secret Weapons, page 12)
2 spring onions (green and white parts), sliced as thinly as possible
shichimi pepper (*shichimi togarashi*) (optional)

If using dried *udon*, bring a medium saucepan half full of water to the boil. Scatter the noodles into the water, then immediately reduce the heat to medium-low and simmer for 15 minutes.

Drain the noodles in a colander set in the sink. Run cold water over them while you rub and swish them with your hand to rinse them. (This process gives the *udon* the desirable firm, chewy texture as well as removing excess starch, making the noodles slippery rather than sticky.) If using fresh *udon*, blanch them by pouring just-boiled water over them in a bowl and leaving them for 5 minutes. Drain and set to one side.

Put the mirin, sake and sugar in a small saucepan and bring to the boil, stirring so the sugar dissolves. Remove from heat and stir in the soy sauce. Allow to cool.

In a medium saucepan, slowly bring the dashi just up to the boil. Stir in the soy sauce mixture. Remove the broth from the heat and keep warm.

Divide the noodles among 4 noodle bowls. Ladle the hot broth over the top so the noodles are swimming and immediately break an egg into each bowl (or add a hot spring egg). Garnish with the spring onions and shichimi pepper to taste and serve immediately, with chopsticks and Chinese spoons.

Beef Pho

Phở Bò (Vietnam)

A scent of charred star anise, of singed cloves and ginger, of fire-blackened garlic and onion, and of the smokiest cassia bark spells absolute comfort and deliciousness to me. It's the heavenly fragrance of pho – the beautiful, delicately spiced, clear yet meaty broth of rice noodle ribbons and fresh, leafy herbs, which is renowned as the national dish of Vietnam. The origins of pho seem to have been lost in the mists of time, but the name apparently comes from the French pot-au-feu – this shares many elements with pho, including adding roasted onion to the broth for colour and flavour. Making pho is a bit of a labour of love, but the process is straightforward and enjoyable and the end result is really worth the effort.

Such a medley of colours, textures, flavours and scents is rarely found, and a bowl of steaming pho is a true joy to lift your soul on a chilly day.

Serves 4–6 | Takes 40 minutes to make, 2 hours 10 minutes to cook

For the spices
- 2 cassia bark sticks or cinnamon sticks
- 3 star anise
- 6 cloves
- 2 tbsp coriander seeds

For the broth
- 2 medium onions, halved (skin still on)
- 7.5cm knob of fresh root ginger (skin on)
- 1kg beef bones (half oxtail bones, half knuckles with marrow)
- 1 x 500g piece of stewing beef such as brisket
- 3 tbsp fish sauce, plus extra to garnish
- 2 lumps of rock sugar or 2 tbsp soft dark brown sugar
- 1 tbsp black peppercorns

To serve
- 200g beef sirloin or fillet steak
- 400g dried narrow, flat rice noodles (*banh phở*, if possible)

To garnish
- 2 medium onions, shaved thinly, soaked in cold water for 30 minutes and drained
- 250g beansprouts, topped and tailed
- small bunch of spring onions (white and green parts), slivered
- sprigs of fresh coriander and mint, plus (if possible) fresh Thai basil and sawtooth herb (culantro/*ngò gai*)
- lime wedges
- fresh red chillies, sliced
- sriracha chilli sauce (though Thai, this is essential and a Vietnamese favourite)
- hoisin sauce

First, toast the spices by tossing them all together in a hot, dry frying pan over a high heat for 1–2 minutes until fragrant. Remove from the heat and set the spices to one side in the pan.

For the broth, char the onions and ginger until the skin blisters all over and goes black, either by setting them on a foil-lined baking tray and blow-torching them or grilling them (under a high heat), or by holding them directly over a gas flame with tongs (be careful and wear oven gloves when doing this). This will take just a few minutes. Let the onions and ginger cool, then peel, removing the blackened bits. Rinse and set to one side.

Put the beef bones and stewing beef in a stockpot or large saucepan with 2 litres cold water. Bring to the boil, then boil briskly for about 10 minutes until scum rises to the surface. Discard the cooking water, then rinse the meat and wash the pot.

Return the meat to the pot and place back on the stove. Add the charred onions and ginger, the toasted spices, the fish sauce, sugar and peppercorns, plus about 2 litres cold water – add enough water so that the ingredients are completely submerged. Bring to the boil and boil briskly for 10 minutes, then reduce the heat and leave to simmer, uncovered, for about 2 hours until the meat is tender. Top up the water if the liquid level ever drops below the ingredients.

Meanwhile, prepare the steak and garnishes. Chill the steak in the freezer for 30 minutes (to make slicing easier), then slice it super-thin. Put all the garnishes into separate dishes on the table.

When the broth is nearly ready, put the rice noodles into a heatproof bowl, generously cover with just-boiled water and leave to soak for 20 minutes. Drain, untangle and set to one side.

When the broth is ready, remove the stewing beef, cut it into bite-sized pieces and set to one side. Strain the broth into a clean pan and discard all the bits, then season the broth to taste by adding more fish sauce or sugar if you think it needs it.

Now you're ready to dish up. Divide the noodles among 4–6 serving bowls and top with pieces of stewing beef and thin slices of raw steak. Bring the strained broth back to a brisk boil, then, while it's still bubbling, put a few ladlefuls into each bowl so the noodles are swimming and the raw beef slices poach gently. Hand the bowls round, telling people to help themselves to the garnishes, and dig in.

Chicken Pho

Phở Ga (Vietnam)

Don't be misled – chicken pho is every bit as delectable as its big brother beef pho. I like to make it when I want the same flavour profile as beef pho, but with a slightly lighter touch. At the table, it's fun to tweak the toppings to your heart's content – perhaps a little more slivered onion, a touch more mint and a good dash of sriracha chilli sauce.

Serves 4–6 | Takes 30 minutes to make, 2 hours to cook

400g dried narrow, flat rice noodles (*bánh phở*, if possible)

For the spices
2 cassia bark sticks or cinnamon sticks
3 star anise
6 cloves
2 tbsp coriander seeds

For the broth
2 medium onions, halved (skin still on)
7.5cm knob of fresh root ginger (skin on)
1 whole chicken, about 1.5kg
6 cloves garlic, peeled
3 tbsp fish sauce, plus extra to garnish
4cm chunk of rock sugar or 2 tbsp soft dark brown sugar
1 tbsp cracked white peppercorns
stems from a small bunch of fresh coriander, tied together with string
1½ tbsp salt

To garnish
Pickled Chillies (Secret Weapons, page 12)
250g fresh beansprouts, topped and tailed
2 medium onions, shaved thinly, soaked in cold water for 30 minutes, then drained
small bunch of spring onions (white and green parts), slivered
sprigs of fresh coriander and mint, plus (if possible) fresh Thai basil and sawtooth herb (culantro/*ngò gai'*)
lime wedges
fresh red chillies, sliced
sriracha chilli sauce
hoisin sauce

First, toast the spices by tossing them all together in a hot, dry frying pan over a high heat for 1–2 minutes until fragrant. Remove from the heat and set the spices to one side in the pan.

For the broth, char the onions and ginger until the skin blisters all over and goes black, either by setting them on a foil-lined baking tray and blow-torching them or grilling them (under a high heat), or by holding them directly over a gas flame with tongs (be careful and wear oven gloves when doing this). This will take just a few minutes. Let the onions and ginger cool, then peel, removing the blackened bits. Rinse well.

Place the chicken in a stockpot or large saucepan. Add the charred onions and ginger, the toasted spices, and all the other ingredients for the broth, plus about 2 litres cold water –enough to completely submerge the ingredients. Cover with a lid and bring to the boil, then turn the heat down to low and poach the chicken for 45 minutes until the meat is tender.

Lift out the chicken; discard the skin and pick the meat off the bone. Tear (rather than cut) the meat into large strips and set to one side. Return the bones to the stockpot and simmer for a further 1½ hours, with the lid slightly askew so that steam can escape.

When the broth is nearly ready, put the rice noodles into a heatproof bowl, generously cover with just-boiled water and leave to soak for 20 minutes. Drain, untangle and set to one side. Put all the garnishes into separate dishes on the table.

When the broth is ready, strain it into a clean pan and discard all the bits. Taste the broth and season by adding more fish sauce or sugar if you think it needs it.

Now you're ready to dish up. Divide the noodles among 4–6 noodle bowls and top with the chicken strips. Bring the broth back to a brisk boil and then, while it's still bubbling, put a few ladlefuls into each bowl so the noodles are swimming. Hand the bowls round, tell people to help themselves to the garnishes and dig in.

Cook's Tips
Chicken pho is very popular, but the classic version is beef pho, and this is my favourite too, as you can add flank, brisket, sirloin, tendon (an acquired taste that I love, which you can get in the freezer section of any oriental supermarket) and even tripe, as well as addictively bouncy beef balls.

Tempura Crumb Udon
Tanuki Udon (Japan)

If you're a fan of the Studio Ghibli films, you may have seen Pom Poko, a sort of environmental-awareness film starring Japanese racoon dogs known as *tanuki*. According to Japanese folklore, the legendary *tanuki* is mischievous and jolly, but gullible and absent-minded. It is also a master of disguise and shape-shifting (they use leaves to shape-shift, which is why goods from Tom Nook's shop in the video game *Animal Crossing* turn into leaves). They're also reputed to have enormous testicles, which you'll see on the *tanuki* statues often found at the entrances to Japanese restaurants (they bring good luck)... This dish is known as *Tanuki Udon* because the creatures are apparently fond of tempura crumbs.

Serves 4 | Takes 30 minutes to make, 20 minutes to cook

400g dried udon noodles or 600g fresh (*yude udon*)
150ml mirin
150ml sake
1 tbsp caster sugar
100ml light soy sauce
1.5 litres Dashi (page 9)
4 slices of any Japanese fishcake (*kamaboko*, *naruto* or *chikuwa*)
2 spring onions (green and white parts), sliced as thinly as possible
2cm knob of fresh root ginger, peeled and grated
2cm chunk of fresh white radish (daikon/mooli), peeled and grated (optional)
handful of dried nori seaweed strips (optional)
shichimi pepper (*shichimi togarashi*) (optional)
Tempura Crumbs (Secret Weapons, page 13)

If using dried *udon*, bring a medium saucepan half full of water to the boil. Scatter the noodles into the water, then immediately reduce the heat to medium-low and simmer for 15 minutes. Drain the noodles in a colander set in the sink. Run cold water over them while you rub and swish them with your hand to rinse them. (This process gives the *udon* the desirable firm, chewy texture as well as removing excess starch, making the noodles slippery rather than sticky.) If using fresh *udon*, blanch them by pouring just-boiled water over them in a bowl and leaving them for 5 minutes. Drain and set to one side.

Put the mirin, sake and sugar in a small saucepan and bring to the boil, stirring so the sugar dissolves. Remove from heat and stir in the soy sauce. Leave to cool.

Pour the dashi into a medium saucepan and bring just up to the boil. Stir in the soy sauce mixture and the fishcake slices. Remove from the heat and keep warm.

Divide the noodles among 4 noodle bowls and ladle the hot broth over the top so the noodles are swimming and the fishcake slices are divided equally. Garnish with the spring onions, ginger, daikon, nori and shichimi pepper to taste. Add the tempura crumbs and serve immediately, with chopsticks and Chinese spoons.

Spicy Lemongrass Beef Noodles

Bún bò Huế (Vietnam)

This is by far my favourite Vietnamese noodle soup – so much so that I find myself ordering it whenever I'm at a Vietnamese restaurant, however appealing the rest of the menu might be. In fact, at City Caphe, a lunchtime haunt in London, they barely ask me what I want any more, so notorious is my craving. The dish comes from Huế in central Vietnam, a city that is famous for the cooking style of the former royal court, so it is sometimes known as Imperial Beef Noodles. It's spicy, sour, salty and sweet – an explosion of flavours in every mouthful.

Serves 4 | Takes 30 minutes to make, 3 hours 30 minutes to cook

300g dried thick, round rice noodles (Vietnamese *bún* or Guilin rice vermicelli)

For the broth
1 medium onion (skin on)
2cm knob of fresh root ginger (skin on)
500g oxtail pieces
500g pork bones
1 x 1kg piece of boneless beef brisket or shin
1 pork hock
12 stalks lemongrass, trimmed of woody bits, bruised and tied in 3 bunches with string
$\frac{1}{4}$ fresh pineapple (cut crossways), peeled, or 4 tinned pineapple rings
2 tbsp Vietnamese fine shrimp paste (*mắm ruốc*)
50g chunk of rock sugar
1 tbsp salt
3 tbsp fish sauce

For the spice paste
2 tbsp groundnut oil
1 tbsp annatto seeds
2 stalks lemongrass, trimmed of woody bits and finely chopped
2 cloves garlic, finely chopped
6 Asian shallots or 1 banana shallot, finely chopped
2 tbsp Vietnamese fine shrimp paste (*mắm ruốc*)
1 tbsp chilli flakes

To garnish
2 medium onions, shaved thinly, soaked in cold water for 30 minutes and drained
handful of sliced banana blossom (optional)
100g beansprouts, topped and tailed
sprigs of fresh Vietnamese coriander (laksa leaf/*rau răm*)
sprigs of fresh coriander
lime wedges
4 fresh red finger chillies, thinly sliced

For the broth, char the whole onion and ginger until the skin blisters and goes black all over, either by sitting them on a foil-lined baking tray and blow-torching them or grilling them (under a high heat), or by holding them directly over a gas flame with tongs (be careful and wear oven gloves when doing this). The charring will take just a few minutes. Let the onion and ginger cool, then peel and remove the blackened bits. Rinse thoroughly. Set to one side.

Combine the oxtail and pork bones in a stockpot or large saucepan and pour in enough water to cover. Bring to the boil and bubble for 5 minutes, then drain. Rinse the bones with cold running water, then place them in the washed stockpot.

Add 2 litres of water, the beef, pork hock, charred onion and ginger, and the remaining broth ingredients except the fish sauce to the stockpot. Bring to the boil and bubble away for 5 minutes, skimming off any scum that rises. Then turn the heat down to low and simmer until all the meat is cooked: the pork hock should take about 1 hour (at which point you should add the spice paste – see below) and the beef about 3 hours. Remove the meats when they are done and leave to cool before slicing (discard the bone from the hock).

While the broth is simmering, make the spice paste. Heat the oil in a frying pan on a medium-high heat and add the annatto seeds. When all the colour seems to have leached from the seeds into the oil, turning it red (this will take a couple of minutes), remove the seeds. Now add the rest of the ingredients for the spice paste and stir-fry for 4–5 minutes until fragrant. Remove from the heat.

When you take the pork hock out of the broth, add the spice paste and the fish sauce to the simmering broth and stir well. Continue simmering to finish cooking the beef.

Put the rice noodles in a large heatproof bowl and generously cover with just-boiled water. Leave to soak for 1 hour. Drain in a colander and rinse thoroughly with running cold water, then set to one side in the colander so that any residual water can continue to drain.

When you're ready to serve, reheat the noodles by placing the colander in your sink and pouring a kettleful of boiling water over them. Divide the noodles among 4 bowls. Top with the sliced beef and pork hock.

Fish out the pork bones, bunches of lemongrass, ginger and onion from the stockpot and discard. Ladle the simmering broth and oxtail pieces into the bowls of noodles. Top with the shaved onions and banana blossom, if using. Serve with chopsticks and Chinese spoons, with the beansprouts, herbs, lime wedges and chilli on the side.

Duck and Bamboo Shoot Noodles

Bún Măng Vit (Vietnam)

Bún Măng Vit, or **Bún Vịt Nấu Măng**, shows the divide between the north and south of Vietnam – the Southern style here uses dried bamboo shoots, which have a wonderfully unusual flavour and texture. If you want to try the Northern style, simply substitute 400g preserved bamboo shoots, which you can get in a tin or packet.

Serves 4 | Takes 45 minutes to make, 2 hours 30 minutes to cook, plus overnight soaking the day before

80g dried bamboo shoots
300g dried thick, round rice
   noodles (Vietnamese *bún*)
1 whole duck or 4 duck
   thighs/quarters, 1–1.5kg
   total weight
1 tbsp groundnut oil
2 tsp salt
3cm knob of fresh root ginger,
   peeled and smashed
4cm chunk of rock sugar or
   2 tbsp soft dark brown sugar
1 tbsp fish sauce
8 spring onions

For the ginger-fish sauce dip
3cm knob of fresh root ginger,
   peeled and finely chopped
Vietnamese Dipping Sauce
   (Secret Weapons, page 13)

To serve
Fried Shallots (Secret
   Weapons, page 11)
sprigs of fresh Vietnamese
   coriander (laksa leaf/*rau
   răm*), shredded
sprigs of fresh coriander

The day before, you need to rehydrate the dried bamboo shoots. Rinse them well under cold running water, squeezing them, to remove some of the mustiness. Put them in a bowl, cover generously with water and leave to soak overnight.

The next day, rinse and squeeze the bamboo again, then submerge in a saucepan of water. Bring to the boil and boil for 20 minutes. Drain and rinse out the saucepan, then add fresh water and boil the bamboo shoots for another 20 minutes. The bamboo will expand to look like actual pieces of bamboo cane; it will be bendy and will have lost the funky dried smell. Drain, rinse and leave to cool, then chop or tear into 4cm pieces, discarding any woody bits. Set to one side.

Put the rice noodles in a large heatproof bowl and generously cover with just-boiled water. Leave to soak for 1 hour. Drain in a colander and rinse thoroughly with running cold water, then set to one side in the colander so that any residual water can continue to drain.

Remove as much of the fat from the duck as possible (save it for rendering and making roast potatoes), then rinse the duck thoroughly. Pat it dry with kitchen paper.

Heat the oil in a stockpot or large saucepan on a medium heat and brown the duck all over (if any duck fat renders, again save it). Now add 1 teaspoon salt and 3 litres water. Cover with a lid and bring to the boil, skimming off any scum that rises, then turn the

heat down to medium-low. Add the smashed ginger and sugar. Leave to simmer, uncovered, for 45 minutes until the duck is tender.

Remove the duck and allow to cool, then take the meat off the bones in pieces as complete as possible, including the skin. Slice the meat into neat 1cm-wide slices, keeping the skin on, and set to one side (reserve the bones).

Add the duck bones, the other teaspoon salt, the fish sauce and bamboo shoots to the stockpot of broth. Bring back to boil, then reduce the heat to medium-low and simmer for another 45 minutes, again skimming off any scum that rises.

Meanwhile, chop the white parts and the start of the green parts of the spring onions into 5cm pieces. Julienne the rest of the green parts. Set to one side. Mix together the ginger and Vietnamese dipping sauce. Set aside.

When the broth has finished simmering, discard the bones and the smashed ginger, and add the spring onion white parts to blanch them.

Now reheat the noodles by placing the colander in your sink and pouring a kettleful of boiling water over them. Divide the noodles among 4 noodle bowls and top with slices of duck meat. Add ladlefuls of the simmering broth and bamboo shoots to the bowls. Garnish with fried shallots and the spring onion green parts. Serve with chopsticks and Chinese spoons, and the ginger-fish sauce dip and herbs on the side.

Crab, Tomato and Omelette Noodles

Bún Riêu Cua (Vietnam)

This Vietnamese rice vermicelli soup can be made with prawns (*Bún Riêu Tom*), whelks (*Bún Riêu Oc*) or, as in this case, crab. Traditionally, freshwater paddy crabs are pounded (with the shell still on) to a fine paste that is then sieved. The crab juices are used as a base for the soup and the rest of the paste is used as the base for the crab omelette. However, these days even Vietnamese chefs will use tinned 'crabmeat in spices', which is readily found in oriental and Asian supermarkets.

Serves 4–6 | Takes 1 hour to make, 1 hour 30 minutes to cook

400g dried thick, round rice noodles (Vietnamese *bún*)

For the broth
200g dried shrimps
3 tbsp groundnut oil
1 medium onion, sliced
6 litres pork stock
3 tbsp fish sauce
4 tbsp Tamarind Juice (Secret Weapons, page 13)
1 tbsp Vietnamese fine shrimp paste (*mắm ruốc*)
4cm chunk of rock sugar or 2 tbsp soft dark brown sugar
1 x 400g tin plum tomatoes
6 ripe medium tomatoes, quartered
10 medium-sized fried beancurd puffs (*tau pok*), halved

For the crab omelette
1 banana shallot, peeled
1 x 320g tin 'crabmeat in spices' (see Cook's Tip)
200g fresh or tinned crabmeat
100g minced pork
1 tsp salt
4 eggs, beaten

To serve
sprigs of fresh mint and coriander, plus (if you can get them) Vietnamese balm (*kinh giới*) and shiso
1 cos or iceberg lettuce, or water spinach stems (*rau muống*), shredded
200g beansprouts, topped and tailed
lime wedges
Fresh Chilli Garlic Sauce (Secret Weapons, page 11)

Put the rice noodles in a large heatproof bowl and generously cover with just-boiled water. Leave to soak for 1 hour. Drain in a colander and rinse thoroughly with running cold water, then set to one side in the colander so that any residual water can continue to drain.

Put half of the dried shrimps in a bowl, cover with plenty of just-boiled water and leave to soak for at least 30 minutes (do not drain).

Heat the oil in a large stockpot on a high heat. Add the onion and the rest of the dried shrimps and fry for 5 minutes until fragrant. Pour in the stock and the liquid from the soaked shrimps (leaving the shrimps in the bowl), cover with a lid and bring to the boil. Remove the lid and turn the heat

down to medium, then add the fish sauce, tamarind juice, shrimp paste, sugar and tinned tomatoes. Simmer for 1 hour.

Meanwhile, finely chop the soaked shrimps with the shallot in a blender or food processor. Spoon into a large bowl and add both types of crabmeat, the minced pork and salt, then add the eggs and mix thoroughly to make a thick batter – this is for the crab omelette.

Bring the broth in the stockpot back to the boil and add the fresh tomato quarters and tofu puffs. Then slowly pour in the omelette batter – it will sink to the bottom, then rise back up to the top in a 'cloud'. Break up the cloud gently into smaller patties.

Divide the noodles among 6 noodle bowls. Ladle the broth into each bowl, making sure that you add some of the crab omelette patties, tofu puffs and tomato quarters to each. Let people help themselves to herbs, lettuce, beansprouts, lime wedges and chilli garlic sauce.

Cook's Tip
The crab that gives the dish its proper flavour comes in squat tins labelled *Gia Vi Cua Bun Rieu* with the English label translated variously as 'Mince [sic] Crab in Spices' or 'Crabmeat in Spices'. You'll find this in oriental and Asian supermarkets in the condiments section. You can also use the prawn version known as *Gia Vi Nau Bun Rieu* ('Mince [sic] Prawn in Spices') for a slightly sweeter flavour.

Tom Yum Soup Noodles

(Thailand)

Tom Yum, that soup of wonders, that spicy restorative, that Thai dish which even gave its name to a Tony Jaa action film for reasons that still escape me (imagine if *Mission Impossible 3* was renamed Mulligatawny!). There's a lot of controversy about what constitutes an authentic Tom Yum (sometimes spelled Tom Yam) – should it contain tomatoes?; what type of mushrooms if any?; prawns or chicken? – and it seems some recipes throw in everything but the proverbial kitchen sink. I've even seen people use coconut milk, which makes it too close to *Tom Kha Ghai* for my liking. And any version with pineapple is going straight in the sin bin.
I have to admit that I used to err on the side of plenty, but I found it became too much of a muddy jumble. So these days I like to strip it down and use as few ingredients as possible. This gives a fresher, lighter, sharper taste – a broth that almost sparkles with clarity.

Serves 4 | Takes 20 minutes to make, 10 minutes to cook

500g fresh mussels (in shell)
2 stalks lemongrass, trimmed of woody bits
2 fresh, red bird's eye chillies
200g dried rice vermicelli noodles
6 kaffir lime leaves, roughly torn (use fresh if possible; frozen will do)
1 tsp salt
1 tbsp palm sugar or soft dark brown sugar
1 lime, cut into 4 wedges
4 tbsp fish sauce
handful of fresh coriander leaves

Clean the mussels by washing them well under cold running water. De-beard and de-barnacle them, if necessary, and discard any that do not shut when tapped sharply on the worktop. Set to one side.

Chop the lemongrass and chillies into fine rings (deseed the chillies if you don't like things too hot). Set to one side.

Cook the rice noodles according to the packet instructions, then drain and set to one side.

Put the lemongrass, lime leaves, salt, sugar and 1 litre cold water into a large saucepan and bring to the boil. Add the mussels, cover with a lid and simmer for about 5 minutes until the mussels have opened up (discard any unopened mussels).

Meanwhile, divide the cooked rice noodles among 4 large soup bowls. Squeeze a wedge of lime into each bowl and add a tablespoonful of fish sauce. Sprinkle the sliced chillies into the bowls. Ladle some mussels and soup into each bowl, garnish with the coriander and serve immediately.

Cook's Tip

I've used mussels here, but you could also use fresh clams in shell, the classic prawns in shell (*tom yum goong*), a mixture of seafood or chunks of skinless, boneless chicken (preferably thigh meat for flavour and juiciness). Whichever you use, adjust the cooking time accordingly – you want to poach the seafood or meat gently, to preserve its character and let the flavours sing.

Boat Noodle Soup

Kuay Teow Rua (Thailand)

At one time, Bangkok was known as the Venice of the East because it was criss-crossed by an extensive network of river canals called *khlong*. These canals were used for transportation and for floating markets, where this cheap and cheerful dish would be served from boats by vendors. While it can still be found on the boats of Bangkok's remaining floating markets, the best boat noodles are to be found at 'boat noodle alley' near Victory Monument in Bangkok.

Serves 4 | Takes 30 minutes to make, 3 hours 20 minutes to cook

200g Asian beef balls, halved
400g dried narrow, flat rice noodles (*bánh phở*, if possible)

For the broth
$1/2$ bunch of fresh coriander, with stems and roots
1kg boneless beef shin
2 litres beef stock
2 cinnamon sticks
4 star anise
6 cloves
4 cloves garlic, smashed
1 medium onion, quartered
2cm knob of fresh root ginger, peeled and smashed
2cm knob of fresh galangal, peeled and smashed
2 stalks lemongrass, trimmed of woody bits and bruised
4 kaffir lime leaves (fresh or frozen)

6 dried Thai chillies

For the broth seasoning
2 tbsp Indonesian sweet soy sauce (*kecap manis*)
2 tbsp fish sauce
1 tsp light soy sauce
1 tbsp dark soy sauce
1 tbsp chilli flakes
1 tbsp palm sugar or soft dark brown sugar
1 tsp salt
$1/2$ tbsp freshly ground black pepper
$1/2$ tbsp freshly ground white pepper

To serve
100g beansprouts, topped and tailed
handful of baby spinach leaves
Crispy Garlic Oil (Secret Weapons, page 11)
lime wedges
pork rinds
Pickled Chillies (Secret Weapons, page 12)
chilli flakes
freshly ground white pepper

Start with the broth. Pick off the coriander leaves and set aside for the garnish; lightly bruise the stems and roots, then tie them together with string. Put the shin in a stockpot with all the other broth ingredients, including the bundle of coriander stems and roots. Pour in 1 litre of water. Bring to the boil, then turn the heat down to medium-low and simmer for 3 hours, topping up the water when necessary, to keep the ingredients submerged. Lift out the beef, slice it into bite-size pieces and set to one side.

Strain the broth into a clean pan; discard all the solids. Bring back to the boil, then add all the seasoning ingredients and the beef balls. Turn the heat down to medium-low and simmer for 20 minutes.

Meanwhile, put the rice noodles into a heatproof bowl, generously cover with just-boiled water and leave to soak for 20 minutes. Drain, untangle and divide among 4 noodle bowls.

Top the noodles with the sliced beef and beansprouts, then ladle the simmering broth over the noodles, reheating everything in the process. Make sure everyone gets some beef balls. Add the spinach leaves, scatter chopped coriander leaves on top and drizzle on some garlic oil. Serve with chopsticks and Chinese spoons, with the lime wedges and other condiments on the side.

Chiang Mai Curry Noodles

Khao Soi (Thailand)

A famous dish from Northern Thailand, this was probably influenced by the Burmese dish *Ohn-no Khao Swè*, because Chiang Mai and the surrounding regions have a large Burmese and Shan community, and in fact Chiang Mai was once part of Burma. The name of the dish means 'cut rice' in Thai, but it's suspected that this is just a corruption of the Burmese word for noodles, which is *khao swè*. This may account for the fact that it's generally served with wheat or egg noodles rather than rice. It's a wonderful dish – spicy yet comforting at the same time.

Serves 4 | Takes 35 minutes to make, 1 hour to cook

300g dried standard thick wheat noodles (*lo mein*) or egg noodles

For the spice paste
4 dried red chillies, stalks removed
4 cardamom pods
1/2 tsp coriander seeds or 1 tsp ground coriander
1 tbsp garam masala or other curry spice mix
2 banana shallots, peeled
4 cloves garlic, peeled
2cm knob of fresh root ginger, peeled
2cm knob of fresh turmeric root, peeled, or 1/2 tsp ground turmeric
stems from 1/2 bunch of fresh coriander (keep the leaves for the garnish)

For the broth
2 tbsp groundnut oil
4 boneless, skinless chicken thighs, about 500g total weight, cut into strips
600ml unsweetened coconut milk
600ml chicken stock
3 tbsp fish sauce
1 tbsp palm sugar or soft dark brown sugar
1 tbsp light soy sauce
1 tbsp dark soy sauce

To serve
200g preserved mustard greens, drained and shredded
1 banana shallot, shaved thinly, soaked in cold water for 30 minutes, then drained
2 spring onions (green and white parts), julienned
leaves from 1/2 bunch of fresh coriander, chopped
crispy noodles (see Cook's Tip)
Fried Shallots (Secret Weapons, page 11)
lime wedges
chilli flakes

First make the spice paste. Toast the dried chillies, cardamom pods, coriander seeds and garam masala in a small, dry frying pan on a high heat for 2–3 minutes until fragrant. Tip into a blender or food processor and add the other spice paste ingredients with 2 tablespoons water. Grind to a smooth paste.

Cook the noodles according to the packet instructions. Drain in a colander and rinse thoroughly with cold water, then set to one side in the colander so that any residual water can continue to drain.

Next make the broth. Heat the oil in a stockpot or large saucepan on medium-high heat. Add the spice paste and fry for 2–3 minutes until fragrant. Add the chicken and toss to coat the strips in the paste, then stir-fry for 3–4 minutes until the meat is no longer pink. Add the rest of the broth ingredients. Bring to the boil, then turn down the heat to medium-low and leave to simmer for 45 minutes.

When you're ready to serve, reheat the noodles by placing the colander in your sink and pouring a kettleful of boiling water over them.

Divide the noodles among 4 noodle bowls and add a ladle or two of the simmering broth. Top with mustard greens, both types of shallot, spring onions, chopped coriander leaves and crispy noodles. Serve with chopsticks and spoons, with the lime and chilli on the side.

Cook's Tip
To make the crispy noodles, follow the method for the Secret Weapon Crispy Rice Noodles on page 11, but use cooked standard thick wheat noodles (*lo mein*) or cooked egg noodles instead of rice noodles. Pat them dry before frying so the oil doesn't spit.

Pork Ball and Glass Noodle Soup

Gaeng Jued Woon Sen (Thailand)

This is a light and peppery dish that feels like it's doing you good – in fact, it's thought to help cure colds and sore throats (compare the Jewish 'penicillin' that is chicken soup). It is often served with more vegetables, such as dried and fresh mushrooms and pak choi, but this stripped-down version is a classic.

Serves 4 | Takes 30 minutes to make, 30 minutes to cook

For the pork balls

stems and roots from ¼ bunch fresh coriander (keep the leaves for the garnish) or ½ teaspoon coriander seeds, crushed
300g minced pork
2 cloves garlic, finely chopped
1 tsp rice flour
1 tsp light soy sauce
1 tsp freshly ground white pepper

For the soup

1 litre chicken stock
100g dried mung-bean thread noodles
1 tsp white peppercorns, crushed
2 cloves garlic, crushed
1 tbsp groundnut oil
2 tbsp fish sauce
1 tsp palm sugar or soft dark brown sugar
pinch of salt

To garnish

Fried Shallots (Secret Weapons, page 11)
leaves from ¼ bunch fresh coriander
2 spring onions (green and white parts), finely sliced
1 red finger chilli, finely sliced
juice of 1 lime

If using fresh coriander stems and roots, grind them to a fine paste in a pestle and mortar or blender. Combine the coriander paste (or crushed seeds) with all the remaining ingredients for the pork balls in a bowl and mix thoroughly. Form into small meatballs, each about the size of a 50-pence piece. Set to one side on a tray, spacing them apart so they do not stick together.

Bring the chicken stock to the boil in a large saucepan. Turn the heat down to medium and add the pork balls one at a time (cook in batches so you don't crowd the pan). Simmer for a few minutes – the pork balls will rise to the top of the stock when they are cooked. Remove with a slotted spoon and set to one side while you cook the remaining pork balls. When they are all cooked, return them to the pan and add the noodles and remaining soup ingredients. Bring back to the boil, then simmer for 5 more minutes.

Divide among 4 noodle bowls, making sure everyone has some pork balls and noodles. Top with fried shallots, coriander leaves, spring onions and chilli. Squeeze some lime juice into each bowl and serve, with chopsticks and Chinese spoons.

Spicy Yellow Noodles

Mee Soto (Malaysia/Indonesia/Singapore)

Soto Ayam is a spicy yellow chicken soup, mainly found in Indonesia but popular in neighbouring countries. When noodles are added to the dish, it's known as *Mee Soto*. This is another of those carb-heavy delights – as well as noodles, it's served with potatoes and cubes of cooked rice known as *lontong*!

Serves 2 | Takes 35 minutes to make, 1 hour to cook

200g dried rice vermicelli noodles

For the spice paste
1/2 tsp coriander seeds
1/2 tsp cumin seeds
1/2 tsp white peppercorns
6 Asian shallots or 1 banana shallot, peeled
4 cloves garlic, peeled
1cm piece of fresh turmeric root, peeled, or 1/4 tsp ground turmeric
1cm piece of fresh root ginger, peeled
2 candlenuts or macadamia nuts

For the broth
2 tbsp groundnut oil
1 cinnamon stick
3 cloves
2 cardamom pods
2 star anise
4 boneless, skinless chicken thighs, about 500g total weight, cut into strips
1 stalk lemongrass, trimmed of woody bits, smashed and then tied in a knot
3cm knob of fresh galangal, peeled and smashed
6 kaffir lime leaves (fresh or frozen)
1 x 400ml tin coconut milk
400ml chicken stock
juice of 1/2 lime

To serve
rice cubes (*lontong*) (see Cook's Tip)
2 small waxy potatoes, boiled, peeled and sliced
4 hard-boiled eggs, quartered
Fried Shallots (Secret Weapons, page 11)
handful of fresh celery leaves, chopped
Indonesian Chilli Paste (*sambal oelek*) (Secret Weapons, page 12)
lime wedges

Put the noodles into a heatproof bowl, generously cover with just-boiled water and untangle the noodles with a fork, then leave to soak for 15 minutes. Drain in a colander and rinse with running cold water. Set to one side in the colander so the noodles can continue to drain.

Next make the spice paste. Toast the coriander seeds, cumin seeds and white peppercorns in a dry frying pan on a high heat for 2–3 minutes until fragrant. Tip into a blender or food processor and add the other spice paste ingredients and 2 tablespoons water. Grind to a smooth paste.

For the broth, heat the oil in a large saucepan on a high heat and fry the cinnamon, cloves, cardamom and star anise for a minute until fragrant. Add the spice paste and stir vigorously, then fry for a few more minutes until the paste becomes fragrant and turns brown. Now add the chicken strips and fry for another minute until the meat is coated in the paste and changes colour.

Finally, add the other broth ingredients, except the lime juice, plus 200ml water. Bring to the boil, then turn the heat down to medium-low, cover the pan and simmer for 45 minutes. At the end of this time add the lime juice and stir.

When you're ready to serve, divide the noodles between 2 noodle bowls and top with some rice cubes, potatoes and eggs. Ladle the hot broth into the bowls and sprinkle with fried shallots and celery leaves. Serve immediately, with chopsticks and Chinese spoons, and chilli paste and lime wedges on the side.

Cook's Tip

Lontong is traditionally made by par-boiling rice and then packing it tightly into a banana leaf. The parcel of compressed rice is then boiled until the rice finishes cooking. Once the rice has cooled, it's cut up into cubes. A much easier way to make the rice cubes is to simply take some cooked rice while it's still warm, and pack it as tightly as possible into a clean, dry ice-cube tray. When cool, pop out the rice cubes and use immediately, or keep in the fridge for up to a day.

Curry Laksa

Laksa Lemak (Malaysia)

There seem to be as many variations of laksa, a noodle soup from the Peranakan culture, as there are stars in the sky. These differences aren't so surprising when you discover that laksa has been co-opted as the national dish of both Malaysia and Singapore, and that it originally came from the Peranakans who are ethnically Chinese. The version that is most familiar is Malaysian *Laksa Lemak*. Also known as *Nyonya Laksa*, it is a type of curry laksa with a particularly rich and sweet coconut gravy. It's my favourite type of laksa as it's comforting yet spicy, perfect when the world seems a bit grey and you need a little kick.

Serves 4–6 | Takes 25 minutes to make, 1 hour to cook

For the spice paste (*rempah*)
- 6 dried red chillies
- 2 tbsp coriander seeds
- 2 tbsp shrimp paste (*belacan*)
- 10 candle nuts or macadamia nuts
- 5cm knob of fresh galangal, peeled
- 5cm knob of fresh root ginger, peeled (see Cook's Tip)
- 6 cloves garlic, peeled
- 6 banana shallots, chopped
- 3 stalks lemongrass, trimmed of woody bits
- 5cm knob of fresh turmeric root, peeled, or 1 tsp ground turmeric
- 60g dried shrimps

For the laksa gravy
- 12 raw king prawns (in shell, plus heads too if possible)
- 4 tbsp groundnut or other vegetable oil
- 2 x 400ml tins coconut milk
- 1 tbsp palm sugar or soft dark brown sugar
- 1 tbsp fish sauce
- 200g ready-made fishcake, sliced
- 200g ready-made fish balls, halved
- 12 large fresh mussels (in shell), cleaned
- 200g prepared fresh squid, cut into rings

To serve
- 250g dried rice vermicelli noodles
- 250g dried thin egg noodles (*bakmi*) or standard thick wheat noodles (*lo mein*)
- handful of beancurd puffs (*tau pok*) (optional)

To garnish
- 4 hard-boiled eggs, peeled and cut into wedges
- 250g fresh beansprouts, topped and tailed
- 1/2 cucumber, deseeded and sliced into matchsticks
- sprigs of fresh Vietnamese coriander (laksa leaf, *rau răm*), shredded
- small bunch of spring onions, slivered
- fresh red chillies, sliced
- lime wedges

First, make the spice paste. Place the dried red chillies in a bowl and cover with boiling water, then leave to soak for about 10 minutes. Drain.

While the chillies are soaking, toast the coriander seeds by tossing them in a hot, dry frying pan over a medium-high heat for 1–2 minutes until fragrant. Remove to a plate. Wrap the *belacan* in some foil and heat it in the same dry frying pan for a few minutes until fragrant.

Put the drained chillies, toasted coriander seeds and *belacan* in a blender or food processor with all the other ingredients for the spice paste and blend to a smooth paste (or use a pestle and mortar if you're willing to put in some elbow grease). Set to one side.

Next, peel the prawns for the laksa gravy, but keep the shells and heads. Set the prawns aside.

Heat the oil in a deep saucepan over a medium-high heat and fry the spice paste until the oil separates (the oil should be red) – this takes about 15 minutes. Add the prawn shells and heads to the pan and fry briefly until they turn pink. Add the coconut milk, sugar, fish sauce and 500ml cold water and stir to mix. Bring gently to the boil, then simmer for 20 minutes. This is your laksa gravy.

While the gravy is simmering, put the rice noodles into a heatproof bowl, generously cover with just-boiled water and leave to soak for 20 minutes; drain, untangle and set to one side. At the same time, cook the egg noodles according to the packet instructions, then drain and set to one side.

Remove the prawn shells and heads from the laksa gravy using a slotted spoon and discard. Add the fishcake slices and fish balls.

Bring gently back to the boil and simmer for 10 minutes until they are cooked through.

Add the prawns, mussels, squid rings and beancurd puffs, if using, to the laksa gravy and cook over a high heat for about 10 minutes until piping hot and all the seafood is cooked (the mussels will have opened up; discard any that are still closed).

Divide the 2 types of noodles among bowls for serving. Ladle the laksa gravy and seafood on to the noodles, making sure each bowl has a bit of everything. Scatter some garnishes on top of each bowl and eat.

Tamarind Fish Laksa

Asam Laksa (Malaysia/Indonesia/Singapore)

This is the other main type of laksa dish, though not as well known worldwide as Curry Laksa. Asam, or Assam, Laksa is named after the Malay words for tamarind and a type of mangosteen, which are used to give the stock its sour note. There are further variations within Asam Laksa itself, such as Penang Laksa and Ipoh Laksa (both named after regions in Malaysia), but the recipe below is a classic.

Serves 6–8 | Takes 1 hour to make, 1 hour 30 minutes to cook

500g dried thick, round rice noodles (there are specific *laksa* noodles which are difficult to find; or you could use Vietnamese *bún* or Guilin rice vermicelli)

500g fresh whole mackerel, scaled, gutted and cleaned

4 pieces of dried mangosteen peel (*asam keping*) (optional – see Cook's Tip)

2 torch ginger buds (*bunga kantan*), sliced (optional – see Cook's Tip)

large handful of fresh Vietnamese coriander leaves (laksa leaf/*rau răm*)

75ml Tamarind Juice (Secret Weapons, page 13)

2 tbsp palm sugar or soft dark brown sugar

2 tbsp fish sauce

1 tsp salt

For the spice paste

30g shrimp paste (*belacan*)

8 dried red chillies, rehydrated in water and then deseeded

8 fresh red finger chillies, deseeded

10 Asian shallots or 3 banana shallots, peeled

3 stalks lemongrass (white part only), trimmed of woody bits and smashed

2cm knob of fresh turmeric root, peeled, or ½ tsp ground turmeric

1cm piece of fresh galangal, peeled

2 torch ginger buds (*bunga kantan*) (optional – see Cook's Tip)

1 tbsp groundnut oil

To garnish

1 Asian or Lebanese cucumber, or ½ regular cucumber, peeled, deseeded and julienned

large handful of fresh mint leaves

1 red onion, shaved thinly, soaked in cold water for 30 minutes, then drained

4 fresh bird's eye chillies, thinly sliced

½ fresh pineapple, peeled, cored and cut into matchsticks

2 torch ginger buds (*bunga kantan*), sliced (optional – see Cook's Tip)

For the sweet prawn sauce

3 tbsp black prawn paste (*hae ko/petis udang*) mixed with 3 tbsp hot water

Put the noodles in a large heatproof bowl and generously cover with just-boiled water. Leave to soak for 1 hour. Drain in a colander and rinse thoroughly with running cold water, then set to one side in the colander so that any residual water can continue to drain.

Bring 1.5 litres of water to the boil in a large saucepan or stockpot. Add the fish, then turn down the heat to medium-low and simmer for 15 minutes. Transfer the cooked fish to a large bowl and leave to cool. Strain the fish stock into a clean stockpot and add the mangosteen peel and ginger buds, if using, plus the Vietnamese coriander leaves. Simmer on a medium-high heat for 15 minutes.

While the broth is simmering,

remove the flesh from the fish and discard the bones. Flake the fish. Add to the broth, cover the pan and reduce the heat to medium-low. Leave to simmer for 30 minutes.

Meanwhile, make the spice paste. Wrap the shrimp paste in foil and either roast in the oven at 180°C/Gas Mark 4 for 15 minutes, or toast with a blowtorch/over a gas flame using tongs (wear oven gloves!). Cool, then unwrap and place in a blender or food processor. Add the other ingredients for the spice paste, except the oil, and grind until smooth. Heat the oil in a wok or frying pan on a medium-high heat and stir-fry the spice paste for 6–7 minutes until fragrant.

Discard the Vietnamese coriander leaves from the simmering broth. Add the spice paste and tamarind juice, and stir gently to combine. Simmer for a further 15 minutes, then add the sugar, fish sauce and salt.

When you're ready to serve, reheat the noodles by placing the colander in your sink and pouring a kettleful of boiling water over them. Divide the noodles among 4 noodle bowls and top with all the garnishes plus a spoonful of the sweet prawn sauce. Ladle the broth into the bowls and serve immediately, with chopsticks and Chinese spoons.

Cook's Tip
Torch ginger buds, or ginger flowers, and mangosteen peel are said to give this laksa an essential extra dimension, but as they cannot be sourced in the UK without difficulty, don't worry about leaving these ingredients out! Tamarind will do the job just as well.

Himalayan Noodle Soup

Thukpa (Nepal/Tibet)

Thukpa is the Tibetan word for 'noodle', which has come to refer to a simple noodle soup of meat and vegetables. It's popular in Tibet, where a version called *Thenthuk* uses mutton and hand-made noodles – this is similar to the Central Asian dish *Lagman* – as well as in Nepal, where a heartier, spicier curried broth is the norm. It's also found in Bhutan where buckwheat noodles are used, and the parts of India that border the Himalayas – hence Himalayan noodle soup.

Serves 4 | Takes 15 minutes to make, 45 minutes to cook

2 tbsp groundnut oil
1.5 litres chicken or vegetable stock
2 skinned chicken quarters or ¹/₂ chicken (on the bone), about 750g total weight
400g dried narrow, flat rice noodles (*bánh phở*, if possible)
1 tsp caster sugar
1 carrot, julienned
handful of cauliflower florets
¹/₂ red pepper, deseeded and sliced
50g French beans, trimmed
100g baby spinach leaves
juice of ¹/₂ lime
salt and pepper to taste
handful of fresh coriander leaves, chopped

For the spice paste

1 tbsp mustard seeds
¹/₂ tsp Sichuan peppercorns
¹/₂ tsp black peppercorns
1 tsp cumin seeds
2 fresh green finger chillies, stalks removed
4 very ripe plum tomatoes
1 small onion, peeled
2 spring onions
2 cloves garlic, peeled
2cm knob of fresh root ginger, peeled
2cm knob of fresh turmeric root, peeled, or ¹/₂ tsp ground turmeric
pinch of garam masala

First make the spice paste. Toast the mustard seeds, Sichuan and black peppercorns and cumin seeds in a dry frying pan on a medium-high heat for 3–4 minutes until fragrant. Tip into a blender or food processor and add the rest of the spice paste ingredients. Grind to a smooth paste.

Heat the oil in a large saucepan on medium-high heat. Add the spice paste and stir-fry for 6–7 minutes until fragrant. Pour in the chicken stock and stir well. Bring to the boil, then turn the heat down to medium-low and add the chicken pieces. Leave to simmer for 20 minutes until tender.

Meanwhile, put the rice noodles into a heatproof bowl, generously cover with just-boiled water and leave to soak for 15 minutes. Drain, untangle and set to one side.

Remove the chicken from the broth and take the meat off the bone. Return the bones to the broth. Tear or chop the meat into pieces and set to one side.

Bring the broth back to the boil, boil briskly for 10 minutes and then discard the bones. Add the sugar, carrot and cauliflower.
Turn the heat down to medium-low and simmer for 1–2 minutes, then add the red pepper and French beans. Simmer for another 1–2 minutes.

Divide the noodles among 4 bowls and top with the chicken. Add the spinach to the broth and stir to wilt, then squeeze in the lime juice and season with salt and pepper. Ladle the broth and vegetables over the noodles. Garnish with coriander and serve, with chopsticks and Chinese spoons.

Meatball and Gourd Noodle Soup

Misua at Patola (Philippines)

Misua (also spelled *miswa* or *mee sua*) is a thread-like wheat noodle that signifies long life in Chinese culture. It's been firmly embraced by Pinoys, and there are various *misua* dishes in Filipino cuisine. One of the most famous is the wonderfully named *Misua Bola Bola*, which means 'meatball noodles'. This is a popular variant of that dish made with luffa aka loofah – yes, the same thing you use to scrub yourself in the bath, which in its fresh state is a sweet and tender vegetable that absorbs the broth beautifully.

Serves 2 | Takes 30 minutes to make, 45 minutes to cook

For the meatballs
2 tbsp groundnut oil
1 small carrot, finely chopped
1 medium onion, finely chopped
6 cloves garlic, finely chopped
1 egg, beaten with 1 tbsp water and 1 tsp cornflour
300g minced pork
150g peeled raw prawns, peeled, deveined and finely chopped
1 tsp salt
$\frac{1}{2}$ tsp freshly ground black pepper

For the soup
750ml chicken stock
1 medium luffa (or you could use winter melon or bottle gourd or even a large deseeded cucumber), peeled and cut into large chunks
1 tbsp caster sugar
1 tbsp fish sauce
100g thread-like salted wheat noodles (*misua*) or 150g dried rice vermicelli
1 tsp salt
1 tsp freshly ground black pepper

To serve
Crispy Garlic Oil (Secret Weapons, page 11)
4 spring onions (green and white parts), julienned
handful of fresh Chinese celery leaves, chopped

Heat 1 tablespoon oil in a stockpot or large saucepan on a medium-high heat. Add the carrot and fry for 3–4 minutes until soft. Transfer to a large mixing bowl and set to one side. Add the remaining oil to the pot and heat on a medium-high heat, then fry the onion and garlic for 3–4 minutes until fragrant.

Spoon half of the fried onion and garlic into the bowl with the carrots (leave the rest in the pot and set to one side). Allow the fried onion, garlic and carrot in the bowl to cool down completely before adding half the egg mix plus the rest of the meatball ingredients. Mix together thoroughly. Set to one side.

Now add the chicken stock and 1 litre of water to the fried onion and garlic in the stockpot and bring the boil. Keeping this broth at a rolling boil, use a tablespoon to scoop out balls of the meatball mixture and drop them into the pot. When they're cooked, they will float to the top – this will take 4–5 minutes. When all the meatballs are floating, turn the heat down to medium and simmer for 15 minutes.

Add the luffa, sugar and fish sauce and cook for 4–5 minutes until the luffa is tender. Now add the noodles and simmer for a further 10 minutes before adding the salt and pepper.

Drizzle the rest of egg mix in a circular motion over the soup. Once the egg has set lightly, dish up into 4 soup bowls, making sure you divide the meatballs, chunks of luffa and noodles equally. Drizzle garlic oil over the top and scatter some spring onions and celery leaves on each bowl. Serve immediately, with spoons and forks.

Beef Noodle Soup

Niu Rou Mian (Taiwan)

This particular beef noodle soup is a Taiwanese dish of Chinese origin, though various versions exist throughout Asia. It's so beloved in Taiwan that it's considered a national dish – the city of Taipei even holds an International Beef Noodle Festival every year, where the dish is celebrated, and chefs and restaurants compete for the honour of 'best beef noodle' in Taiwan.

Serves 2 | Takes 20 minutes to make, 2 hours 5 minutes to cook

500g boneless beef brisket, shin or short rib, cut into large chunks
2 medium onions, quartered
2cm knob of fresh root ginger, peeled and sliced
2 plum tomatoes, quartered, or 200g tinned plum tomatoes
150g dried thin egg noodles (*you mian*)

For the spice paste

2 tbsp groundnut oil
2cm chunk of rock sugar, shaved, or 1 tbsp soft dark brown sugar
3 tbsp Chinese rice wine or dry sherry
1 tbsp chilli bean paste
4 cloves garlic, finely chopped
1cm piece of fresh root ginger, peeled and finely chopped
4 star anise
2 tbsp Sichuan peppercorns, crushed
1 tbsp grated orange zest
1 tbsp cayenne pepper

To season

3 tbsp Chinese black vinegar
1 tbsp toasted sesame oil
3 tbsp light soy sauce
6 tbsp dark soy sauce

To serve

2 baby pak choi, leaves separated
4 tbsp Sichuan preserved vegetables (*zha cai*), chopped
2 spring onions (green and white parts), thinly sliced
1 fresh red finger chilli, thinly sliced

Put the beef in a saucepan with the onions and ginger, generously cover with water and bring to the boil. Turn the heat down to medium-low and leave to simmer for 30 minutes.

Meanwhile make the spice paste. Heat the groundnut oil in a frying pan on a high heat, then add the ingredients in list order. Mix together, then stir-fry for 1–2 minutes until fragrant.

Discard the onions and ginger from the broth, then add the spice paste and stir. Top up with cold water so everything is submerged by a couple of centimetres. Bring to the boil. Add the tomatoes, then reduce the heat to medium-low and simmer for $1\frac{1}{2}$ hours.

While the broth is simmering, cook the noodles according to packet instructions; drain and set to one side. Blanch the pak choi by pouring just-boiled water over them and then draining straight away.

When you're ready to serve, divide the noodles between 2 noodle bowls. Bring the broth back to the boil and add the seasonings, then ladle with the beef over the noodles. Top with the blanched pak choi, preserved mustard vegetables, spring onions and chilli. Serve with chopsticks and Chinese spoons.

Burmese Fish Chowder

Mohinga (Burma)

My father's family hails from Mandalay, so whenever we visited Burma, we'd make a 15-hour overnight train journey up from Yangon to see them all. On our bleary-eyed arrival, we'd be whisked to my grandparents' house for bowl after bowl of *Mohinga*. A bounty of piquant textures and tastes, *Mohinga* is a breakfast of fish chowder and rice vermicelli, renowned as the national dish of Burma.

Serves 6–8 | Takes 30 minutes to make, 2 hours 45 minutes to cook

600g dried rice vermicelli noodles

For the broth
5 tbsp gram flour
2 tbsp rice flour
200g tinned mackerel in brine (see Cook's Tip)
100g tinned sardines in oil
500ml fish stock
2 large onions, quartered
handful of shredded banana blossom (optional)
2 tbsp fish sauce

For the spice paste
4 cloves garlic, peeled
3cm knob of fresh root ginger, peeled
2 stalks lemongrass, trimmed of woody bits
stems from a small bunch of fresh coriander (keep the leaves for the garnish)
6 tbsp groundnut oil
1 tbsp medium chilli powder
1 tbsp ground turmeric
1 tsp hot paprika
1 tsp freshly ground black pepper

To serve
2 tbsp groundnut oil
200g ready-made fishcake, sliced
Burmese-style Onion Fritters (*kyet-thun kyaw*), (Secret Weapons, page 10)
Yellow Split-pea Crackers (*bè gyun kyaw*), (Secret Weapons, page 13)
4 white cabbage leaves, shredded
hard-boiled egg wedges
leaves from a small bunch of fresh coriander, chopped
lime wedges
fish sauce
Chilli Oil (Secret Weapons, page 11)
Crispy Garlic Oil (Secret Weapons, page 11)

Toast the gram flour and rice flour by tossing in a dry frying pan on a medium-high heat for 5–6 minutes until fragrant. (Watch like a hawk – the flours can catch and turn black in seconds.) Leave to cool, then whisk with 500ml cold water in a bowl or jug. Set this flour solution to one side.

Next make the spice paste. Grind the garlic, ginger, lemongrass and coriander stems in a blender or food processor to a smooth paste. Heat the oil in a stockpot on a medium-high heat, add the paste and the rest of the spices and fry, stirring, for 3–4 minutes until fragrant.

Add the mackerel and sardines to the stockpot along with the oil and brine from the tins. Mash the fish with a potato masher or a fork until smooth, and stir to combine with the spice paste. Add the flour solution as well as the fish stock. Bring to the boil, then turn the heat down to medium and simmer vigorously for 30 minutes.

Now add the quartered onions, the banana blossom, if using, and 2 litres of water. Turn the heat down to low and simmer for a further 2 hours.

Meanwhile, put the noodles into a heatproof bowl, generously cover with just-boiled water and untangle them with a fork, then leave to soak for 15 minutes. Drain in a colander and rinse with cold water. Set to one side in the colander so they can continue to drain.

Heat the 2 tablespoons oil in a frying pan on medium heat. Add the fishcake slices and fry for 5 minutes until they smell cooked. Set to one side.

When ready to serve, stir the fish sauce into the soup. Divide the noodles among 6–8 pasta plates and ladle the soup on top. Garnish with the fishcake, onion fritters, chunks of split-pea cracker, shredded cabbage, egg and chopped coriander leaves. Serve with soup spoons or metal Chinese spoons, with lime wedges, fish sauce, chilli oil and garlic oil on the side.

Cook's Tip
Mohinga is usually made with small river catfish known in Burmese as *nga gyi*, *nga ku* and *nga yunt*, but a combination of tinned mackerel and sardines can successfully match the flavour of authentic *Mohinga*.

Pork Noodle Hotpot

Kyay-Oh (Burma)

This Burmese dish is named after the copper pot that it would traditionally be cooked in. Its other name is *Dakwet-byohk*, which means 'boiled in one pot', for the manner in which the dish is cooked. If you have a steamboat (ie an electric hotpot) you can turn *Kyay-oh* into a party dish: prep all the ingredients in advance, then let everyone cook for themselves at the table. Some people like to have the broth on the side and the noodles and toppings lightly stir-fried together – this variant is called *Kyay-oh Hsi-Jet*.

Serves 4 | Takes 45 minutes, 2 hours 30 minutes to cook

300g dried rice vermicelli noodles
200g pig intestines (available from oriental and Asian supermarkets), cleaned thoroughly (optional)
200g ready-made fish balls
200g pork liver, thinly sliced

For the broth
200g pork bones
1cm piece of fresh root ginger, peeled and smashed
$1/4$ tsp MSG or 1 tbsp Marigold bouillon powder
1 tbsp caster sugar
1 tsp salt
1 tsp black peppercorns, crushed

For the meatballs
300g minced pork
1 tbsp tapioca flour
1 egg white
$1/2$ tsp salt
1 tsp black peppercorns, crushed

To serve
200g choy sum, separated into leaves
200g silken tofu, drained and cut into 2cm cubes
8 quail's eggs, soft-boiled, cooled and peeled
4 spring onions (green and white parts), thinly sliced
Crispy Garlic Oil (Secret Weapons, page 11)
toasted sesame oil
fish sauce
Pickled Chillies (Secret Weapons, page 12)
Fresh Chilli Garlic Sauce (Secret Weapons, page 11)

Put the noodles into a heatproof bowl, generously cover with just-boiled water and untangle them with a fork, then leave to soak for 15 minutes. Drain in a colander and rinse with cold water. Set to one side in the colander so they can continue to drain.

If using the intestines, submerge them in a saucepan of cold water. Bring to the boil, then turn the heat down and simmer for 45 minutes. Drain the intestines, rinse thoroughly and set to one side.

While the intestines are simmering you can make the broth. Put the pork bones in a stockpot and add enough water to cover. Cover the pot and bring to the boil. Drain the bones and rinse in cold running water, then put them back into the washed stockpot. Add the ginger, MSG, sugar, salt, pepper and 2 litres of water. Cover with a lid and bring to the boil, then reduce the heat to medium-low. Uncover the pot and simmer for $1^{1}/_{2}$ hours.

Meanwhile, combine the ingredients for the meatballs in a large bowl and mix together thoroughly.

Discard the ginger from the broth. Bring it back to the boil, then add the fish balls and pork liver. Let them cook for 1–2 minutes before scooping them out with a slotted spoon and setting to one side.

Bring the broth back to the boil again. Keeping it at a rolling boil, use a tablespoon to scoop out balls of the meatball mix and drop them into the broth. Don't crowd the pan (cook in batches). When they're cooked, the meatballs will float to the top. Scoop them out with a slotted spoon and set to one side. Make the rest of the meatballs in the same way.

Add the choy sum to the broth and blanch for a minute. Scoop out with a slotted spoon and set to one side. Keep the broth simmering.

Divide the noodles among 4 bowls. Top with choy sum, intestines (if using), meatballs, liver, fish balls, silken tofu and quail's eggs. Now ladle the steaming broth into each bowl, reheating everything in the process.

Garnish with spring onions and drizzle with garlic and sesame oils. Serve immediately, with chopsticks and Chinese spoons, and fish sauce, pickled chillies and chilli garlic sauce on the side.

Coconut Chicken Noodles

Ohn-No Khao Swè (Burma)

This is arguably the best-known Burmese dish, as it is generally considered the predecessor of the famous Northern Thai noodle dish, *Khao Soi*. *Ohn-no Khao Swè* literally means 'coconut milk noodles', but the protein used is generally chicken, hence my paraphrase of Coconut Chicken Noodles. This is a wonderfully subtle, lightly curried dish, a little like laksa but without whacking you in the face – the focus is on texture as much as flavour. The Burmese way is to adjust seasoning to taste, by adding more fish sauce, squeezing over more lime juice or sprinkling on more chilli at the table.

Serves 4–6 | Takes 20 minutes to make, 40 minutes to cook

4 tbsp vegetable oil

3 medium onions, finely chopped

1cm piece of fresh root ginger, peeled

4 cloves garlic, peeled

2 spring onions

2 tbsp gram flour

2 tbsp fish sauce

¼ tsp MSG or 1 low-salt vegetable stock cube or 1 tbsp Marigold bouillon powder

250g dried standard thick wheat noodles (*lo mein*)

2 eggs

2 banana shallots or 1 small red onion, very thinly sliced

4 skinless, boneless chicken thighs, about 500g total weight, cut into small strips

2 tbsp sweet paprika

200ml coconut milk

To serve

Crispy Rice Noodles (Secret Weapons, page 11)

Chilli Oil (Secret Weapons, page 11)

lime wedges

Heat 1 tablespoon oil in a large saucepan or stockpot, add the onions and cook gently for about 10 minutes until translucent. Take a tablespoonful of the cooked onions out of the pan and add to the ginger, garlic and spring onions, then grind the lot together in a blender or food processor to form a rough paste. Set to one side.

Whisk the gram flour with 100ml cold water, then add to the pan of cooked onions. Add the fish sauce and the bouillon. Bring to a simmer then top up with 500ml cold water. Bring the broth back to a simmer, then keep it simmering gently.

Meanwhile, cook the wheat noodles according to the packet instructions; drain. Soft-boil the eggs, then drain and cool in cold water. Once cool, peel and slice into wedges. Set aside with the noodles. Slice the shallots finely then soak in a bowl of cold water (see Cook's Tips) until you are ready to serve, then drain.

Heat the remaining 3 tablespoons oil in a wok or frying pan, add the ginger/garlic/spring onion paste and stir-fry over a high heat for a couple of minutes. Add the chicken strips and 1 tablespoon of the paprika and stir-fry for about 5 minutes until the chicken is cooked and browned.

Stir the coconut milk and the remaining paprika into the pan of simmering broth. Tip in the stir-fried chicken mixture, bring back to a simmer and cook for 10 minutes. At this stage the broth can be cooled and kept in the fridge for 48 hours or frozen, if you like (see below).

Divide the cooked wheat noodles among pasta bowls, then ladle the hot chicken broth over. Top with the sliced shallots, the egg wedges and the crispy rice noodles. Add another dash of fish sauce to each serving, and serve with chilli oil and fat wedges of lime for squeezing.

Cook's Tips

The shallots (or red onion) should be sliced as thinly as possible (so that each slice is translucent) and then immediately left to soak in cold water until you are ready to serve. The soaking removes the astringent 'raw' taste, but also keeps the slices crisp, which is important in this dish. When you are ready to garnish your noodles, quickly drain the shallot slices thoroughly and use immediately.

The chicken broth freezes well and can be kept for up to 1 month. Thaw, then reheat gently but thoroughly until piping hot.

Smoky Mushroom and Glass Noodle Soup

Kyar-zun Hin or Kyar-zun Jet (Burma)

My mother's family is from Mogok, which borders the mountainous Shan State in Burma. Her brothers decided to stay there, so whenever we visited, we'd undertake a 6-hour journey by pick-up truck up a narrow, winding mountain path from Mandalay. Halfway up the mountain, we'd pause at a little village called Shwenyaungbin (Golden Banyan) to stretch our legs and for the driver to have a rest. The smouldering smell of wood burning marked this recognised truck stop where we'd draw our tiny stools closer to the fire and indulge in *Kyar-zun Hin* aka *Kyar-zun Jet*, an intense smoky broth packed with sweet, charred shrimps, earthy wood-ear mushrooms and slippery bean-thread noodles. With a sprinkle of smoke-roasted chilli, a dash of fish sauce and a squeeze of lime, every spoonful warmed us and dazzled our tastebuds.

Serves 4 | Takes 30 minutes to make, 1 hour 15 minutes to cook

500g dried mung-bean thread noodles

For the soup

handful of dried lily flowers
handful of dried wood-ear mushrooms
handful of dried shrimps
2 medium onions, cut into wedges
8 cloves garlic, peeled
2 tbsp tomato purée
1/4 tsp MSG or 1 tbsp Marigold bouillon powder
2 tbsp fish sauce
200g ready-made fish balls, halved

To garnish

8 quail's eggs or 4 duck eggs, soft-boiled, cooled, peeled and cut into wedges
chilli flakes
2 medium onions, shaved thinly, soaked in cold water for 30 minutes and drained
handful of fresh coriander leaves, chopped
lime wedges

Tie the lily flowers into knots. Put them in a heatproof bowl with the wood-ear mushrooms, generously cover with just-boiled water and leave to soak for 15 minutes until soft. Do not drain, but snip the mushrooms into smaller pieces with scissors. Set to one side.

Toast the dried shrimps in a hot dry frying pan for 8–10 minutes until almost black. Tip the toasted shrimps into a large, deep stockpot and add the onion wedges, garlic, tomato purée and 1 litre water. Bring to the boil, then simmer for 1 hour.

Add the mushrooms and lily flowers (including the water they were soaking in) to the soup. Pour in another 1 litre of water and add the MSG and fish sauce. Bring the soup back to the boil, then add the fish balls and reduce the heat to medium. Simmer for 5 minutes. Add the noodles and remove from the stove – the noodles will cook in the residual heat.

When you're ready to serve, bring the soup back to the boil, then dish up into 4 noodle bowls, making sure every bowl has a bit of everything. Garnish with the eggs, chilli flakes, shaved onions and chopped coriander. Serve with soup spoons or metal Asian soup spoons, with lime wedges on the side.

Phnom Penh Noodles

Ka Tieu (Cambodia)

Also known as *K'tieu, Hu Tieu* and *Kuy Teav*, this is a breakfast dish in Cambodia, thought to have been brought over by Chinese immigrants. It can be found throughout the country, from high-end restaurants to street-hawkers. Its clear and comforting broth with plentiful toppings have made it so popular that it's considered a national dish.

Serves 4 | Takes 15 minutes to make, 3 hours 10 minutes to cook

400g dried tapioca noodles (*hu tieu*)
2 tbsp groundnut oil
250g minced pork
Crispy Garlic Oil (Secret Weapons, page 11)
4 tsp light soy sauce
4 tsp dark soy sauce
4 tsp oyster sauce
12 large cooked prawns, peeled
200g beansprouts, topped and tailed

For the broth
1 medium onion (skin on)
1kg pork bones
handful of dried shrimps, rinsed and soaked in warm water
1 carrot, peeled
2 tbsp sugar
2 tbsp salt
1 x 250g piece of pork belly
2 tbsp fish sauce

To garnish
6 iceberg lettuce leaves, shredded
4 spring onions (green and white parts), finely chopped
large handful of fresh coriander (leaves and stems), shredded
fresh, red bird's eye chillies, sliced into rings
freshly ground black pepper
lime wedges

To make the broth, char the onion until the skin blisters all over and goes black, either by setting it on a foil-lined baking tray and blow-torching or grilling it (under a high heat), or by holding it directly over a gas flame with tongs (be careful and wear oven gloves when doing this). This will take just a few minutes. Let the onion cool, then peel, removing the blackened bits. Rinse and set to one side.

Bring 4 litres water to the boil in a large stockpot. Add the pork bones, shrimps, charred onion, carrot, sugar and salt and return to the boil. Skim off any scum that rises, then reduce the heat and simmer for 1 hour. Add the pork belly and continue simmering for 2 hours so it poaches gently.

Meanwhile, prepare the noodles according to the packet instructions; drain and set to one side.

Remove the pork belly from the broth; slice thinly and set aside. Strain the broth into a clean pan; discard the bones and vegetables. Add the fish sauce to the broth, then set to one side.

Heat the groundnut oil in a large frying pan on a high heat. Add the minced pork and fry for 5 minutes, breaking it into small meat patties as it browns.

Divide the noodles among 4 noodle bowls. Add 1 tablespoon garlic oil and 1 teaspoon each light soy sauce, dark soy sauce and oyster sauce to each bowl and mix through. Next add a few slices of pork belly, a few minced pork patties, 3 prawns and a small mound of beansprouts to each bowl.

Bring the broth back to the boil. As soon as it's bubbling, ladle enough into each bowl so that the contents are covered. Garnish with the lettuce, spring onions, shredded coriander and chillies, plus a few grinds of pepper. Serve immediately, with chopsticks and Chinese spoons, and lime wedges and extra garlic oil on the side.

Persian Noodle Soup

Ash-e-Reshteh (Iran)

Ash-e-reshteh is a Persian dish made with special thin noodles called *reshteh*, a whey called *kashk*, various pulses and lots of green herbs. It's commonly served at celebrations and is often eaten at Persian New Year, because the noodles represent the threads of life and family intertwined.

Serves 4 | Makes 15 minutes to make, 1 hour to cook, plus overnight soaking the day before

150g dried chickpeas
150g dried red kidney beans
2 tbsp groundnut oil
2 medium onions, sliced
5 cloves garlic, sliced
1 tbsp ground turmeric
150g dried lentils
500ml vegetable stock
2 tbsp plain flour, mixed with 50ml water
200g fresh spinach leaves, chopped
200g fresh flat-leaf parsley, chopped
200g spring onions (green parts only), chopped
200g fresh dill, chopped
200g fresh coriander leaves, chopped
400g Persian *reshteh* noodles (or the thinnest wheat noodles you can find, such as linguinetti)
200ml Persian whey (*kashk*) or soured cream
200g fresh mint leaves, chopped
salt and pepper to taste

Put the dried chickpeas and kidney beans in a bowl, cover with plenty of water and leave to soak overnight. Drain and rinse, then set to one side.

Heat the oil in a stockpot or large saucepan on a medium-high heat. Add the onions and garlic with the turmeric and fry for 5–6 minutes until fragrant. Remove half the onions and set to one side. Continue to fry the onions in the pot for another 5–6 minutes until golden brown.

Add the drained pulses, lentils, stock and 500ml water to the stockpot. Bring to the boil and boil briskly for 10 minutes, then turn down the heat and simmer for 15 minutes. Add the flour solution to the soup and mix well, then simmer for a further 10 minutes.

Now add the chopped spinach, parsley, spring onions, dill and coriander. Simmer for 5 minutes before adding the noodles. Simmer for a final 10–15 minutes until the noodles are tender. Season to taste.

Divide the soup among 4 soup bowls. Drizzle over the *kashk* and sprinkle with the reserved fried onions and the mint. Serve immediately, with spoons.

Cook's Tips

This is often made using dried herbs. Try it this way too, using 2 tablespoons each dried parsley, dill, coriander and mint – what the soup will lack in colour and freshness, it will make up for in intensity.

You can substitute tinned pulses for dried in this dish if you want to save time.

Hawaiian Noodle Soup

Saimin (Hawaii)

Saimin is a noodle soup that was developed in the late 1800s when Hawaii was home to plantation workers from across Asia and Europe, so it bears similarities to and shares ingredients with many dishes from those countries, notably Japan's ramen. Its name simply means 'thin noodles' in Chinese, and it's recognised as a state dish by Hawaii because of the historic and cultural significance of its creation. And yes, it contains Spam.

Serves 2 | Takes 15 minutes to make, 15 minutes to cook

150g dried thin egg noodles (*you mian*) or 200g fresh ramen noodles (*chūkamen*)

For the broth
handful of dried shrimps
750ml Dashi (page 9)
50ml mirin
50ml sake
2 tbsp light soy sauce
1 tsp caster sugar

To serve
100g Chinese barbecue pork (*char siu*), sliced
50g tinned Spam, sliced into strips
50g Japanese fishcake (*kamaboko*), sliced
2 hard-boiled eggs, peeled and halved
4 spring onions (green and white parts), julienned

Place the dried shrimps in a heatproof bowl, generously cover with just-boiled water and leave to soak for 15 minutes until soft. Do not drain.

Cook the noodles according to the packet instructions; drain and divide between 2 noodle bowls. Top with the barbecue pork and Spam.

Pour the shrimps and their soaking water into a saucepan. Add the dashi, mirin, sake, soy sauce and sugar plus 100ml water. Bring to the boil, then scoop out the shrimps with a slotted spoon and discard. Add the fishcake, turn the heat down to medium and simmer for 5 minutes. Scoop out the fishcake with a slotted spoon and divide between the noodle bowls.

Bring the broth back to the boil before ladling it into the bowls over the noodles, reheating them in the process. Add the eggs, scatter the spring onions on top and serve immediately, with chopsticks and Chinese spoons.

Lamb and Vegetable Soup with Hand-Pulled Noodles Laghman (Central Asia)

Lamian is a type of Chinese noodle made by stretching, twisting and folding dough into strands. It's normally eaten with mutton. Recipes for *lamian* have been found dating from the 1500s so it's not surprising that it has since travelled across the world and turned up in the form of *Laghman*, which is a popular dish in Central Asia, particularly Kyrgyzstan and Kazakhstan. This method of making noodles is great fun, and reminds me of playing with Plasticine when I was a child!

Serves 4 | Takes 2 hours to make, 2 hours 10 minutes to cook

For the noodle dough
250g plain flour
125ml warm water
$^{1}/_{2}$ tsp salt

For the broth
2 tbsp groundnut oil
2 tsp ground cumin
1 tsp ground coriander
1 tsp ground mace
600g boneless stewing lamb, cut into 2.5cm chunks
3 tbsp tomato purée
2 medium onions, sliced
4 cloves garlic, sliced
1 red pepper, deseeded and sliced
1 fresh red finger chilli, deseeded and sliced
1 litre beef stock
1 x 400g tin plum tomatoes, with juice
2 bay leaves
1 tbsp caster sugar
1 tbsp salt
1 small potato, peeled and diced
200g fresh white radish (daikon/mooli), peeled and diced
1 large carrot, diced
1 tbsp Chinese black vinegar
$^{1}/_{2}$ tsp chilli flakes
salt and pepper to taste

First make the noodles. Combine the ingredients in a bowl and mix to a dough. Leave to rest for 30 minutes. Cut the dough into 4cm cubes. Rub some oil on your hands, then roll each of the pieces of dough on the worktop to make a sausage shape. Leave to rest for 10 minutes.

Now (again with oiled hands) roll the sausages back and forth on the worktop, twisting them, to make fat noodles about 5mm in diameter. Leave them to rest for 30 minutes, then stretch and twist the fat noodles into long thin ones.

Loop the noodles on the worktop, then place your hands inside the loop and lift up the noodles (as if they were a hank or skein of yarn). Pull your hands apart and 'bang' the noodles on the worktop – let them droop slightly between your hands, then slap the drooping part against the worktop – to stretch the noodles even further.

Place your finished noodles on a tray, cover with clingfilm so they don't dry out and set to one side.

Heat the oil in a stockpot or large saucepan on a medium-high heat. Add the cumin, coriander and mace and stir-fry until fragrant.

Add the lamb and fry, turning occasionally, for 5–6 minutes until browned all over. Add the tomato purée, onions, garlic, red pepper and chilli and stir-fry for a further 3–4 minutes until they are softened and fragrant.

Now add the stock, tomatoes and bay leaves to the stockpot. Bring to the boil, then reduce the heat to low, cover with a lid and simmer for $1^{1}/_{2}$ hours.

Meanwhile, cook the noodles in a large pot of boiling salted water, as you would fresh pasta, for about 5 minutes. Drain and set to one side.

Bring the broth back to the boil, then add the potato, white radish and carrot. Turn the heat down to medium-low and simmer, covered, for a further 30 minutes.

Add the black vinegar and chilli flakes to the broth and season with salt and pepper. Divide the noodles among the bowls and ladle the broth over them, making sure everyone gets some lamb and vegetables. Serve immediately, with chopsticks and Chinese spoons.

Chicken and Cauliflower Noodles

(fusion)

The cauliflower is an underrated vegetable – often seen as a flatulent monster only fit to be drenched in cheese sauce. But in this dish, florets of cauliflower are poached very lightly to preserve their crunch and delicate flavour. It's genuinely the best thing you could do with a cauliflower.

Serves 2 | Takes 15 minutes to make, 35 minutes to cook

150g dried broad, flat rice noodles (*ho fun*)

For the broth
200g skinless chicken thighs (on the bone)
handful of fresh coriander stems, finely chopped to a paste (keep the leaves for the garnish)
2 cloves garlic, peeled
¼ tsp MSG or 1 tbsp Marigold bouillon powder
1 tsp caster sugar
200g cauliflower florets

To serve
Burmese Water Pickle (Secret Weapons, page 10)
handful of fresh coriander leaves, chopped
2 spring onions (green and white parts), finely sliced
Fried Shallots (Secret Weapons, page 11)
freshly ground black pepper

Put the noodles in a large heatproof bowl and generously cover with just-boiled water. After a minute, untangle the noodles, then leave them to soak for a further 8 minutes. Drain in a colander and rinse thoroughly under running cold water. Set to one side in the colander so that any residual water can continue to drain.

Now make the broth. Put the chicken, coriander stem paste, garlic, MSG and sugar in a medium saucepan and add enough water to cover. Bring to the boil, then reduce to medium-low heat and simmer for 30 minutes, skimming any scum from the surface. Top up the water when necessary to keep the chicken submerged.

Remove the chicken, take the meat off the bone and pull it into large strips (discard the bones). If making ahead, you can set the chicken and the broth to one side.

When you're ready to serve, divide the noodles between 2 noodle bowls. Top each bowl with half the chicken and 2 tablespoons water pickle.

Bring the broth to the boil, then add the cauliflower florets. Reduce the heat to medium and simmer for 3 minutes. Ladle the broth and cauliflower florets into the noodle bowls. Sprinkle with chopped coriander leaves, spring onions and fried shallots, and grind plenty of black pepper on top. Serve with chopsticks and Chinese spoons.

Ham and Pea Shoot Noodles

(fusion)

For the uninitiated, pea shoots (also called pea tops or pea sprouts) are the heart-shaped, tendrilly leaves of the garden pea plant. Long beloved in Chinese cookery where they are known as *dòu miáo*, they have only recently made an appearance on our shores. The little leaves taste just like the sweetest, freshest peas and are best eaten raw or blanched, in salads and stir-fries. However, it occurred to me that, since peas and ham go so well together in pea and ham soup, I should create a summery riff on the same. As suspected, pea shoots and ham complement each other beautifully in this much lighter (and quicker) version of the traditional soup.

Serves 2 | Takes 5 minutes to make, 8 minutes to cook

1 tbsp groundnut oil
100g cooked ham, diced
500ml vegetable stock
1 tbsp caster sugar
50g frozen garden peas or petits pois
400g fresh udon noodles (*yude udon*)
100g fresh pea shoots

Heat the oil in a large saucepan, add the ham and stir-fry over a high heat for about 5 minutes until the meat is caramelised.

Pour in the stock and add the sugar. With the heat still on high, bring to a rolling boil, then throw in the peas and *udon* noodles. When the peas and noodles are cooked through (this will only take a few minutes), remove from the heat and dish up into 2 noodle bowls.

Divide the pea shoots between the bowls. Let the pea shoots gently wilt in the heat of the noodle soup for a minute before serving.

Silken Tofu, Yuzu and Samphire Noodles
(fusion)

This is another of those comfortingly light dishes that also happens to be vegan. It has its roots in Japanese cuisine (particularly *shojin ryori*, or 'temple food') but has a foot firmly in the West with its garnish of samphire, a British sea vegetable. Its use makes perfect sense however, since samphire shares flavour and textural notes with the seaweeds that are popular in Japan. Yuzu makes the broth sparkle on your tongue – do try to track it down if you can.

Serves 2 | Takes 10 minutes to make, 10 minutes to cook

300g fresh udon noodles (*yude udon*)
750ml vegetable stock
1 tbsp golden caster sugar
350g block of silken tofu, cut into 2.5cm cubes
100g samphire, rinsed in cold water
2 tsp yuzu juice (see Cook's Tip)
2 spring onions (green and white parts), finely chopped
shichimi pepper (*shichimi togarashi*)

Blanch the noodles by pouring just-boiled water over them in a bowl and leaving them for 5 minutes. Drain, then divide between 2 noodle bowls.

Bring the vegetable stock to the boil in a saucepan and add the sugar. Reduce the heat to medium, then add the tofu followed by the samphire. Simmer for 5 minutes.

Dish up into the noodle bowls, making sure the tofu and samphire are divided equally. Add 1 teaspoon yuzu juice to each bowl, then top with spring onions and shichimi pepper to taste. Serve immediately, with chopsticks and Chinese spoons.

Cook's Tip
If you are unable to find yuzu juice, you can substitute 1 teaspoon lime juice mixed with 1 teaspoon orange juice, but it's available in bottles from Waitrose now.

SAUCES

Spicy Sichuan Noodles

Dan Dan Mian (China)

Also known as 'dandan noodles' abroad, this dish was traditionally sold by vendors walking the streets of the Sichuan province in China – it is named for the pole (*dan dan*) that went over their shoulders. Baskets carrying the noodles and the meat sauce were attached at either end of the pole. In Taiwan and the US, sesame paste and/or peanut butter is added to the dish, but this is the classic version.

Serves 2 | Takes 15 minutes to make, 25 minutes to cook

200g fresh Shanghai noodles (*cui mian*), or you can substitute 125g dried standard wheat noodles (*lo mein*) or medium egg noodles
1 tsp groundnut oil

For the stir-fry
4 tbsp groundnut oil
1 tbsp Sichuan peppercorns
200g minced pork
1cm piece of fresh root ginger, peeled and finely chopped
2 cloves garlic, finely chopped
4 tbsp Sichuan preserved vegetables (*zha cai*) or Tianjin preserved vegetables (*dong cai*), chopped

For the sauce
1 tbsp Chinese rice wine or dry sherry
1 tbsp Chinese black vinegar
1 tsp chilli bean sauce
1 tsp caster sugar
1 tbsp light soy sauce
1 tsp dark soy sauce

For the garnish
Chilli Oil (Secret Weapons, page 11))
2 spring onions (green and white parts), shredded

Heat the oil in a wok or large frying pan on a high heat. Add the Sichuan peppercorns and fry for 1–2 minutes until fragrant. Scoop out the peppercorns with a slotted spoon and discard.

With the heat still on high, add the minced pork, ginger, garlic and preserved vegetables and stir-fry for 3–4 minutes until the meat is no longer pink. Add the wine, vinegar, chilli bean sauce, sugar and soy sauces and mix thoroughly, then stir-fry for 2–3 minutes, breaking up the meat into small pieces. Add 50ml water and bring the sauce to the boil. Turn the heat down to medium-low and simmer for 15 minutes.

Meanwhile, if using Shanghai noodles, blanch them by pouring just-boiled water over them in a bowl and leaving them for 5 minutes. If using dried noodles, cook according to the packet instructions. Drain, then toss the noodles with the oil to prevent them from sticking together.

Divide the noodles between 2 noodle bowls and top with the pork sauce, chilli oil and spring onions. Serve with chopsticks and Chinese spoons, telling the diners to stir the noodles before eating to make sure the sauce is evenly distributed.

Henan Braised Noodles

Hui Mian (China)

It is said that the first person to eat these braised noodles was Li Shimin, the first emperor of the Tang Dynasty. The story goes that he became sick when he was just a poor soldier and begged for some food from an equally poor woman. She nevertheless took pity on him and, using what little she had, made him some wide wheat noodles by hand and served them in a soup made of bones. This cured the emperor-to-be of his ailment, and when he ascended the throne, he ordered his cooks to record the way the noodles had been made, so that the recipe could be passed down to future generations.

Serves 4 | Takes 1 hour
30 minutes to make, 3 hours
30 minutes to cook

For the noodle dough (see Cook's Tip)
500g strong white bread flour or other high-gluten flour
1 tsp salt

For the broth
300g lamb bones
300g boneless stewing lamb, cut into 2cm cubes
1cm piece of fresh root ginger, peeled and smashed
1 medium onion, quartered
1 tbsp Chinese rice wine or dry sherry
1 tbsp five spice powder
1 sheet of beancurd skin, sliced
handful of dried lily flowers
handful of dried wood-ear mushrooms
50g dried kelp knots (*kombu*) (optional)
100g dried mung-bean thread noodles

To season
1 tbsp Chinese black vinegar
1 tbsp light soy sauce
1 tbsp dark soy sauce
1/2 tsp caster sugar
1/2 tsp salt

To serve
200g choy sum
4 hard-boiled quail's eggs, peeled
toasted sesame oil
handful of fresh coriander leaves, chopped
Chilli Oil (Secret Weapons, page 11)

First make the noodles. Sift the flour and salt into a bowl and make a well in the centre. Slowly add 300ml water to the well, stirring until it comes together as a dough. Transfer the dough to a floured work surface and knead vigorously for 10–15 minutes until smooth. Cover lightly with clingfilm and leave to rest for 30 minutes.

Cut the dough into 8 pieces. Roll each piece into a sausage and brush with oil. Cover with clingfilm again and leave to rest for 15 minutes.

Cut each sausage lengthways in half and place the halves cut side up on a clean work surface. Brush the cut sides with oil. Using your fingers, flatten each sausage to about 3mm thick. Leave to rest for 5 minutes. Meanwhile, bring a large saucepan of water to a rolling boil.

Now brush one of the flattened sausages with more oil. Using your thumbs and forefingers, gently lift up both ends of a sausage, then flip, swing and stretch the dough as thinly as possible so it becomes a flat belt-like noodle about 1 metre long and 3–4cm wide. It should resemble pappardelle. Drop the noodle straight into the pan of boiling water and cook for about 2 minutes; drain in a colander and set to one side. Repeat with the other dough sausages.

Next make the broth. Rinse the bones in plenty of cold water before putting them into a stockpot or large saucepan with 2 litres of cold water. Cover with a lid and bring to the boil, then drain. Rinse the bones again. Place them in the washed stockpot and add another 2 litres of cold water plus the lamb cubes, ginger, onion, rice wine and five spice. Cover and bring to the boil. Remove the lid, then leave to simmer for 3 hours.

While the broth is simmering, put the beancurd skin in a large deep dish or tray, generously cover with just-boiled water and leave to soak for 15 minutes until soft. Drain. Cut into 1cm-wide strips (like tagliatelle noodles) and set to one side.

Tie the lily flowers into knots. Put them in a heatproof bowl with the wood-ear mushrooms and kelp knots, generously cover with just-boiled water and leave to soak for 15 minutes until soft. Do not drain, but snip the mushrooms into smaller pieces in the bowl.

Blanch the choy sum by pouring just-boiled water over them and then draining straight away. Set to one side.

Discard the bones, ginger and onion from the broth. Add the mung-bean thread noodles, the lily flowers, wood ear mushrooms and kelp knots (with their soaking liquid), and the beancurd skin to the stockpot. Bring to the boil again, then turn the heat down to medium-low. Add the seasoning ingredients and leave to simmer gently for 15 minutes.

Reheat your home-made noodles by placing the colander in your sink and pouring a kettleful of boiling water over them. Divide the noodles among 4 noodle bowls and top with the choy sum and quail's eggs. Ladle the simmering broth over the noodles, making sure each bowl has a bit of everything. Drizzle with sesame oil and sprinkle with coriander, then serve immediately, with chopsticks and Chinese spoons, and chilli oil on the side.

Cook's Tips
The story behind these braised noodles is curiously similar to that of Biang Biang Noodles, which tells us that when Qin Shi Huang, the first emperor of the Qin dynasty, was sick one day, his servant got him a cheap bowl of noodles from the street that cured him. The emperor was so enthralled by the noodles and how they were made that he issued a long proclamation about how wonderful Qin, its people and these noodles were, and then took a brush and ink and created a character '*biang*', which included parts of all of the words in his statement (said character containing 57 brush-strokes, and to this day not accepted by most Chinese dictionaries).

Biang Biang Noodles are in fact made in more or less the same way as Henan Noodles, except when you stretch the noodles, you're meant to thwack them against the table – '*biang*' also mimics the noise the noodles make when you do that. Apparently.

If you want to make Biang Biang Noodles, follow the recipe for the noodles above, but instead of serving them in the broth, add the dressing and garnishes from Cold Sesame Noodles (see page 127), plus 1 teaspoon each ground roasted Sichuan peppercorns, fennel seeds, cumin seeds and chilli flakes and some preserved mustard greens.

Ants Climbing a Tree

Ma Yi Shang Shu (China)

A classic Sichuan dish, this consists of mung-bean thread noodles coated in a minced meat sauce. Its colourful name comes from the idea that the morsels of meat clinging to the noodles remind one of ants marching along twigs.

Serves 2 | Takes 25 minutes to make, 15 minutes to cook

200g minced pork
4 dried shiitake mushrooms
200g dried mung-bean thread
  noodles
3 tbsp groundnut oil
3 cloves garlic, finely chopped
1cm piece of fresh root ginger,
  peeled and finely chopped
1 stalk Chinese celery, thinly
  sliced
4 spring onions, white parts
  finely chopped, green parts
  shredded
300ml chicken or vegetable
  stock
1 tbsp toasted sesame oil
2 fresh red finger chillies,
  chopped

For the pork marinade
1 tsp dark soy sauce
2 tsp light soy sauce
2 tbsp chilli bean sauce
1 tsp toasted sesame oil
2 tbsp Chinese rice wine or
  dry sherry
2 tsp golden caster sugar
pinch of cornflour

Combine the minced pork with all its marinade ingredients in a bowl and mix well. Leave to marinate for at least 15 minutes.

Meanwhile, put the shiitake mushrooms in a bowl, generously cover with just-boiled water and leave to soak for 15 minutes until soft. Drain (reserving the soaking liquid) and slice the mushrooms. Set to one side.

Put the noodles in a heatproof bowl, generously cover with just-boiled water and leave to soak for 6 minutes until al dente. Drain in a colander and rinse with plenty of cold water. Cut the noodles into shorter lengths using scissors. Set to one side.

Heat a wok or large frying pan on a high heat and add the oil. When it is hot, add the garlic, ginger and celery and stir-fry for 1–2 minutes until fragrant. Add the pork and its marinade and stir-fry for 4–5 minutes until the meat has browned, breaking it up into small pieces as you go. Turn the heat down to medium, then add the noodles and the spring onion whites and mix well to combine. Stir-fry for a further 1–2 minutes.

Pour in the stock. Bring to the boil, then simmer for 4–5 minutes until the liquid has been absorbed. Serve the noodles in sauce on a platter. Drizzle with sesame oil and sprinkle with the chillies and spring onion greens.

Hot Dry Noodles
Re Gan Mian (China)

Re Gan Mian (or *Reganmian*), literally meaning 'hot dry noodles', is a breakfast dish traditionally sold by street vendors in Wuhan in central China. It seems that the noodles are so-called because they are cooked, mixed with oil and then left to dry before being scalded again and mixed with spices just before eating. Drying them out in this way means they have a chewy texture, which acts as a nice foil against the spicy sauce.

Serves 2 | Takes 45 minutes to make, 5 minutes to cook

150g dried standard thick wheat noodles (*lo mein*)
1 tbsp toasted sesame oil

For the sauce
3 tbsp Chinese sesame paste or tahini
4 cloves garlic, crushed
1 tbsp groundnut oil
2 tbsp light soy sauce
1 tbsp dark soy sauce
1 tbsp Chinese black vinegar
$1/2$ tsp caster sugar
1 tbsp Chiu Chow chilli oil with sediment
$1/4$ tsp salt
1 tbsp boiling water

For the garnish
4 tbsp Sichuan preserved vegetables (*zha cai*), chopped
2 spring onions (green and white parts), thinly sliced
1 tbsp sesame seeds
Pickled Chillies (Secret Weapons, page 12)

Cook the noodles according to packet instructions. Drain in a colander and dress with the sesame oil (mix with your hands), then leave the noodles to dry out in the colander for at least 30 minutes.

Combine all the sauce ingredients in a bowl or jug and whisk vigorously.

When you're ready to serve, reheat the noodles by placing the colander in your sink and pouring a kettleful of boiling water over them.

Tip the noodles into a large bowl, pour the sauce over them and mix thoroughly. Divide between 2 pasta dishes and sprinkle with the preserved mustard vegetables, spring onions, sesame seeds and pickled chillies. Serve with chopsticks.

Lobster Noodles

Lobster Yee Mein (China)

This crowd-pleasing dish is perfect for Chinese New Year and other special occasions – the noodles are known as longevity noodles and bring luck, and the lobster is, of course, a luxury.

Serves 4 | Takes 10 minutes to make, 15 minutes to cook, plus 2 hours live lobster freezing time

1 live lobster (1–1.5 kg) or 2 lobster tails
400g dried thick egg noodles (*yee mein*)
3 tbsp groundnut oil
4cm knob of fresh root ginger, peeled and julienned
4 spring onions (green and white parts), sliced on the diagonal into 2cm pieces
2 tbsp cornflour mixed with 4 tbsp cold water
1 tbsp toasted sesame oil

For the sauce
2 tbsp oyster sauce
1 tbsp light soy sauce
1 tsp caster sugar
1 tbsp Chinese rice wine or dry sherry
1 tbsp toasted sesame oil
salt and white pepper to taste

Kill your lobster. (I'm not going to give instructions, because I am a coward and made my husband do this while I hid in the other room.) Crack the lobster claws gently and chop the lobster (or tails) into 4–5 sections, saving any juices to add to the sauce. Blot the lobster pieces dry with kitchen paper, place in a bowl and set to one side.

Cook the noodles according to the packet instructions. Drain in a colander, rinse with cold water and set to one side in the colander.

Whisk the sauce ingredients together, with salt and pepper to taste, and set to one side.

Heat the groundnut oil in a wok or large frying pan on a high heat. Add the ginger and stir-fry for 2–3 minutes until fragrant, then add the lobster pieces. Move and stir the lobster continually for 2–3 minutes until the shell starts to turn red. Add the white parts of the spring onions and the whisked sauce, and stir to ensure the lobster is well coated. Add the cornflour paste and 100ml water, mix thoroughly and stir-fry for another 2 minutes.

Meanwhile, reheat the noodles by placing the colander in your sink and pouring a kettleful of boiling water over them. Spread the noodles on a serving dish or platter and drizzle with the sesame oil.

Pour the lobster and sauce over the platter of noodles and mix to combine. Garnish with the green parts of the spring onions and serve immediately. Give everyone noodle bowls and chopsticks and tell them to dig in.

Beijing Bolognese

Zha Jiang Mian (China)

This noodle dish, popular throughout China, is known colloquially in US Chinatowns as 'Chinese Spaghetti' or 'Beijing Bolognese' due to the familiar combination of thick noodles and rich meat sauce. The Korean version of the dish is known as *Jajangmyeon*, and you can even buy jars of ready-made 'Jah Jan Mien' sauce (the Americanised name) if you want an easy cheat.

Serves 4 | Takes 20 minutes to make, 30 minutes to cook

400g fresh Shanghai noodles (*cui mian*), or you can substitute 250g dried standard thick wheat noodles (*lo mein*) or medium egg noodles
1 tsp groundnut oil

For the stir-fry
2 tbsp groundnut oil
200g pork belly, finely chopped
200g minced pork
4 cloves garlic, finely chopped
1cm piece of fresh root ginger, peeled and finely chopped
6 spring onions (white parts only; save the green parts for the garnish), finely chopped

For the sauce
100ml Chinese rice wine or dry sherry
4 tbsp yellow soybean sauce
4 tbsp sweet wheat sauce (*tianmianjiang*), or 2 tbsp hoisin sauce mixed with 2 tbsp Indonesian sweet soy sauce (*kecap manis*)
1 tbsp golden caster sugar
2 tbsp light soy sauce
2 tbsp dark soy sauce

To garnish
100g beansprouts, topped and tailed
1 Asian or Lebanese cucumber, or 1/2 regular cucumber, peeled, deseeded and julienned
6 spring onions (green parts only), julienned

Start with the stir-fry. Heat the oil in a wok or large frying pan on a medium-high heat. Add the pork belly, minced pork, garlic, ginger and spring onion white parts and stir-fry for 4–5 minutes until the meat is no longer pink and it all smells fragrant.

Add all the sauce ingredients and mix thoroughly, then stir-fry for a further 2–3 minutes, breaking up the minced pork into small pieces. Add 50ml water and bring to the boil. Turn the heat down to medium-low and simmer the pork sauce for 15 minutes.

Meanwhile, blanch the beansprouts by pouring just-boiled water over them and draining straight away; set to one side. If using Shanghai noodles blanch them by pouring just-boiled water over them in a bowl and leaving them for 5 minutes. If using dried noodles, cook according to the packet instructions. Drain the noodles, then toss with the oil to prevent them from sticking.

Divide the noodles between 2 noodle bowls and top with the pork sauce, cucumber, beansprouts and spring onion greens. Serve with chopsticks and Chinese spoons, telling the diners to stir the noodles before eating to make sure the sauce is evenly distributed.

Pork and Rolled Noodle Stew

Guay Jub (Thailand/Malaysia)

Also called *Kueh Chap* or *Kuay Jaab*, this is a spicy, fragrant stew of pork bits and noodles that curl up and dance as you chase them with your chopsticks. According to the head chef at the excellent restaurant Janetira Thai in London, the broth should be light, sweet, aromatic and salty. Thai people will DIY the taste themselves with condiments at the table.

Serves 4–6 | Takes 20 minutes to make, 2 hours 40 minutes to cook

400g dried square or triangular rice flake noodles (*sen kuay chap*)
1 x 200g piece of pork belly
200g pork ribs, chopped into 4cm pieces
2 pork knuckles
1 tbsp palm sugar or soft dark brown sugar
200g pig intestines (available from oriental and Asian supermarkets)
groundnut oil for deep-frying
4 soft-boiled eggs, cooled and peeled
handful of beancurd puffs (*tau pok*)

For the braising liquid
1/2 bunch of fresh coriander with roots
1 tbsp Sichuan peppercorns, crushed
1 tbsp black peppercorns, crushed
4 star anise
4 cinnamon sticks
4 black cardamom pods
1 tbsp cloves
2cm knob of fresh root ginger, peeled and smashed
6 cloves garlic, crushed
2 tbsp palm sugar or soft dark brown sugar
6 tbsp dark soy sauce
4 tbsp light soy sauce
4 tbsp oyster sauce

To serve
Crispy Garlic Oil (Secret Weapons, page 11)
4 spring onions (green and white parts), sliced thinly
Fresh Chilli Garlic Sauce (Secret Weapons, page 11)

Put the noodles in a large heatproof bowl and generously cover with just-boiled water. After a minute, untangle the noodles, then leave them to soak for another 15 minutes until they curl up into 'rolls'. Drain in a colander and rinse thoroughly with cold water. Set to one side in the colander so that any residual water can continue to drain.

Place the pork belly, ribs and knuckles in a large stockpot with enough cold water to cover. Add the sugar. Bring to the boil, then turn the heat down to medium, cover with a lid and simmer for 1 hour.

Meanwhile, pick the leaves from the bunch of coriander and set aside for the garnish. Crush the coriander roots.

Rinse and clean the intestines in plenty of cold, running water, then blanch by boiling in plenty of water for 5 minutes. Drain, then rinse well again.

Remove the pork belly from the pot and set to one side. Add the pork intestines to the pot along with all the ingredients for the braising liquid including the coriander roots. Top up with enough cold water to submerge everything by 2cm. Bring back to the boil, then turn the heat down to medium and simmer for 1½ hours.

While the broth is simmering, dry the pork belly with kitchen paper. Heat a 5cm depth of oil in a wok or large frying pan on a high heat until you can feel waves of heat rising above it with the palm of your hand. Add the piece of pork belly and deep-fry for 4–5 minutes until golden. Lift out the pork belly and drain on kitchen paper. When it's cool, chop it into chunks and set to one side.

Remove all the meat from the broth and set to one side. Strain the broth into a clean pan. Pick the meat off the knuckles and ribs, and slice up the intestines if necessary. Divide the noodles among 4 bowls and top with the fried pork belly, rib and knuckle meat and intestines. Set to one side.

Bring the broth back to the boil. Add the eggs and beancurd puffs and simmer for 10 minutes so they take on the colour of the broth. Scoop them out with a slotted spoon. Slice the eggs in half, then divide the beancurd and eggs among the bowls.

Ladle the steaming broth into the bowls, reheating the noodles and the meat in the process. Top with garlic oil, spring onions and coriander leaves. Serve with chopsticks and Chinese spoons, and dipping bowls of chilli garlic sauce on the side.

Dai Meat and Tomato Noodles

Kanom Jeen Nam Ngiao/Kao Soi Lao (Thailand/Laos)

This dish seems to come from the Shan people in Burma. It's only found in Northern Thailand and Laos, which have large Shan communities, and contains a special Shan ingredient called *tua nao*. *Kanom jeen* also happens to be a fermented rice vermicelli that came from the Mon people in Burma; the Lao version of this dish favours flat rice noodles. At any rate, I've called this recipe Dai noodles since Dai is the name of the Shan people in Thailand.

Serves 4 | Takes 25 minutes to make, 2 hours to cook

400g dried narrow, flat rice noodles (*bánh phở*, if possible) or dried rice vermicelli noodles

For the pork broth
400g pork spare ribs, chopped into bite-size pieces
1/4 tsp MSG or 1 tbsp Marigold bouillon powder
1 tbsp sugar
1 tsp salt and 1/2 tsp freshly ground white pepper
150g pork blood cubes (available fresh or frozen in oriental and Asian supermarkets) (optional)

For the sauce
10 dried red chillies, soaked in warm water to rehydrate and then deseeded
6 shallots, peeled
6 cloves garlic, peeled
1/2 tsp salt
3 tbsp groundnut oil
1 Shan fermented soybean cake (*tua nao*), crumbled (see Cook's Tip)
200g minced pork
2 tbsp hot chilli powder
1/4 tsp MSG or 1 tbsp Marigold bouillon powder
4 ripe tomatoes, peeled and roughly chopped, or 10 baby plum tomatoes, halved
dried red kapok flower (*dok ngiao*) (optional)

For the garnish
preserved mustard greens, chopped
100g beansprouts, topped and tailed
6 white cabbage leaves, shredded
4 spring onions (green and white parts), thinly sliced
handful of fresh coriander leaves, chopped

To serve
Crispy Garlic Oil (Secret Weapons, page 11)
pork rinds
Deep-fried Dried Red Chillies (Secret Weapon, page 11)
lime wedges

Put the ribs, MSG, sugar, salt and white pepper in a stockpot with enough water to cover. Bring to the boil, then reduce the heat to low, cover with a lid and simmer for 1 hour. Add the pork blood cubes, if using, and simmer for 15 minutes.

While the broth is simmering, make the sauce. Pound the chillies with a pestle and mortar into a smooth paste; scoop out and set to one side. Put the shallots and garlic in the mortar, add the salt and pound into a smooth paste.

Heat the oil in a wok on high. Add the shallot and garlic paste and stir-fry for 2–3 minutes until fragrant. Reduce the heat to medium and keep stir-frying until the paste turns brown, and the oil soaked up by it starts to reappear (in Burmese this is called 'hsi-byun' – 'the oil returns').

Add the chilli paste and stir-fry for a minute, then add the crumbled bean cake and stir-fry for 2–3 minutes. Add the minced pork and stir-fry for another 2–3 minutes, breaking the pork into pieces. Add the chilli powder, MSG and 500ml boiling water. Mix well, then add the tomatoes and kapok flowers, if using, and stir again. Reduce the heat to low and simmer, uncovered, for 30–35 minutes until the sauce thickens.

While the sauce is simmering, put the rice noodles into a heatproof bowl, cover with just-boiled water and soak for 20 minutes. Drain, untangle and divide among 4–6 noodle bowls. Add a ladleful of the meat and tomato sauce to each bowl. Garnish with all the vegetables, then pour a ladleful of the pork broth, spare ribs and blood cubes, over the noodles so they're swimming (or you can serve the broth separately in small soup bowls). Sprinkle with coriander and serve with chopsticks and Chinese spoons, with the garlic oil, pork rinds, fried chillies and lime wedges on the side.

Cook's Tip
You can substitute 1 tablespoon of miso, mashed Japanese fermented soybeans (*natto*) or mashed yellow soybean sauce for the *tua nau*.

Ribbon Noodles with Gravy

Lad Na/Rat Na (Laos/Thailand)

A Chinese-influenced dish popular in Laos and Thailand, this is a sibling to the Malay dish _Wat Tan Hor_. Both use ribbon noodles and vegetables in a rich gravy, and both are utterly moreish.

Serves 4 | Takes 20 minutes to make, 15 minutes to cook

150g dried broad, flat rice noodles (_ho fun_)
400g pork fillet (tenderloin), thinly sliced
2 tbsp groundnut oil
3 tbsp dark soy sauce
4 cloves garlic, finely chopped
2 tsp yellow soybean sauce
200g Chinese broccoli (_kai-lan_), chopped
200g tinned straw mushrooms, drained
Pickled Chillies (Secret Weapons, page 12), to serve

For the pork marinade
1 tsp tapioca flour
1 tsp light soy sauce
1 tsp dark soy sauce
1 tsp caster sugar
1 tsp groundnut oil
pinch each of salt and pepper

For the gravy
750ml chicken or vegetable stock
2 tbsp caster sugar
2 tbsp Indonesian sweet soy sauce (_kecap manis_)
2 tbsp light soy sauce
2 tbsp fish sauce
3 tbsp tapioca flour mixed with 6 tbsp cold water to a paste

Put the noodles in a large heatproof bowl and generously cover with just-boiled water. After a minute, untangle the noodles, then leave them to soak for another 6 minutes until al dente. Drain in a colander and rinse thoroughly with cold water. Set to one side in the colander so that any residual water can continue to drain.

Mix together the ingredients for the pork marinade in a bowl. Add the slices of fillet and leave to marinate for 15 minutes.

Heat 1 tablespoon oil in a wok or deep frying pan on a medium heat. Add the noodles and dark soy sauce and stir-fry for 2–3 minutes until the noodles have absorbed the colour of the soy and turned brown. Remove and keep warm on a serving dish or platter.

Heat the remaining oil in the wok on a high heat and stir-fry the garlic for 1–2 minutes until fragrant. Add the yellow soybean sauce and stir-fry for 30 seconds, then add the marinated pork and stir-fry for 2–3 minutes until it changes colour.

Now add the ingredients for the gravy, except the tapioca paste, and bring to the boil. Add the Chinese broccoli and straw mushrooms and cook for another 2–3 minutes. Turn the heat down to medium. Add the tapioca paste and stir to combine. Season to taste with salt and pepper. Simmer for 5 minutes until the gravy has thickened.

Pour the finished gravy over the platter of warm noodles. Give everyone pasta dishes and spoons and forks to help themselves, and serve with pickled chillies on the side.

Shimeji Mushroom and Shiso Leaf Pasta

Shimeji Shiso Pasuta (Japan)

Wafu pasta, or **wafuu pasuta**, is the slightly bonkers Japanese interpretation of Italian pasta dishes ('**wafu**' meaning 'Japanese-style'). The first time we went to Harajuku in Japan, my husband and I stumbled across a restaurant called Yomenya Goemon, which specialised in the stuff. Its windows showcased plastic versions of each dish they served, and it became clear that as far as toppings were concerned, anything goes. This version bursts with colour and flavour, using bright orange fish roe that pop like salty jewels, meaty shimeji mushrooms and zingy shiso leaf.

Serves 2 | Takes 20 minutes to make, 5 minutes to cook

- 300g dried durum wheat spaghetti (I like De Cecco brand)
- 1 clump of fresh shimeji mushrooms, or 100g fresh shiitake mushrooms, sliced
- 2 fresh green or purple shiso leaves
- 1 tbsp olive oil
- 1 tbsp Japanese soy sauce (**shoyu**)
- 1 tbsp Dashi (page 9)
- 2 tbsp mirin
- 50g salmon roe (**ikura**), flying fish roe (**tobiko**) or red lumpfish roe (see Cook's Tip)
- handful of dried nori seaweed strips
- 2 spring onions (green and white parts), shredded
- shichimi pepper (**shichimi togarashi**), to serve

Cook the spaghetti according to packet instructions. Drain, but reserve 3 tablespoons of the cooking water in a small bowl. Keep the pasta warm.

While the pasta is cooking, slice off 1cm from the base of the clump of shimeji mushrooms; discard this root piece. Break the mushrooms into small clusters. Roll the shiso leaves into a 'cigar' and shred finely. Set to one side.

Heat the oil in a frying pan over a high heat and sear the mushrooms until they brown and crisp slightly – this will take a couple of minutes. Add the soy sauce, dashi, mirin and the reserved pasta cooking water to the mushrooms and sizzle over a high heat for another couple of minutes.

Divide the cooked spaghetti between 2 pasta bowls. Chuck the mushrooms and their cooking sauce over the spaghetti, then scatter the fish roe, nori and shredded shiso and spring onions on top. Sprinkle with some shichimi pepper and serve immediately.

Cook's Tip

Salmon roe (*ikura*) and red lumpfish roe can be found in jars in supermarkets; *ikura* and *tobiko* (flying fish roe) are available fresh from the fish counter in Japanese supermarkets.

Curry Udon

Karē Udon (Japan)

Curry was introduced to Japan during the Meiji era by the British when India was part of the British Empire. As a result, it was generally considered to be Western cuisine, or *yōshoku*, although it's now eaten so widely it's a national dish. Japanese curry sauce is usually made from instant curry roux, which comes in block and powder forms, so there's no shame in using it here. Ready-to-eat curry is even available in retort pouches in Japanese supermarkets – just heat the contents and pour over noodles or rice.

Serves 2 | Takes 15 minutes to make, 20 minutes to cook

3 tbsp groundnut oil
1 medium onion, sliced
1 large carrot, diced
1 medium floury potato, peeled and diced
2 boneless, skinless chicken thighs, about 200g total weight, diced
1 litre Dashi (page 9)
handful of frozen petits pois
2 Japanese curry roux cubes
300g fresh udon noodles (*yude udon*)
2 spring onions (green and white parts), finely sliced
1 fresh red finger chilli, sliced

Heat the oil in a large saucepan on a high heat. Add the onion, carrot and potato and stir-fry for 3 minutes until the onion is fragrant. Add the chicken and stir-fry for another 3 minutes until the meat is opaque.

Now add the dashi and the peas and bring to the boil. Turn the heat down to medium, add the curry roux cubes to the pot and simmer for 10 minutes: the solid curry roux cubes will break down. Then simmer for a further 5 minutes or so, stirring, until the cubes completely melt into the dashi, forming a thick and smooth curry sauce.

While the sauce is simmering, blanch the noodles by pouring just-boiled water over them in a bowl and leaving them for 5 minutes. Drain well.

Divide the noodles between 2 noodle bowls and pour the curry sauce on top. Garnish with the spring onions and chilli and serve immediately, with chopsticks.

Sweet Soy Chicken Noodles

Mie Ayam (Indonesia)

Also called *Bakmi Ayam*, this is a Chinese-Indonesian dish served by restaurants and street-hawkers alike. It consists of yellow wheat-based noodles (*bakmi* in Indonesian) topped with diced chicken (*ayam*) and seasoned with sweet soy sauce, and served with a bowl of chicken broth on the side.

Serves 4 | Takes 25 minutes to make, 1 hour 30 minutes to cook

2 chicken quarters, or ¹/₂ chicken, about 750g total weight
300g dried standard thick wheat noodles (*lo mein*)

For the chicken broth
4 spring onions (white parts only; save the green parts for the garnish), sliced
2 sticks celery, sliced
salt and pepper to taste

For the chicken oil
250ml groundnut oil
4 cloves garlic, sliced
2cm knob of fresh root ginger, peeled and sliced
pinch of white pepper
pinch of ground coriander

For the spice paste
6 Asian shallots or 1 banana shallot, peeled
4 cloves garlic, peeled
2cm knob of fresh turmeric root, peeled, or ¹/₂ tsp ground turmeric
3cm knob of fresh root ginger, peeled

1 tsp ground coriander
4 candlenuts or macadamia nuts
2 tablespoons groundnut oil

For the noodle dressing
2 tbsp light soy sauce
2 tbsp Indonesian sweet soy sauce (*kecap manis*)
2 tbsp Worcestershire sauce

To serve
4 baby pak choi
Fried Dumpling Skins (Secret Weapons, page 11)
4 spring onions (green parts only), julienned
fresh celery leaves, chopped
Fried Shallots (Secret Weapons, page 11)
Fresh Chilli Garlic Sauce (Secret Weapons, page 11)

Remove the skin and bones from the chicken. Dice the chicken meat; smash the chicken bones; and snip the chicken skin into 2cm pieces. Set them all to one side.

Now make the chicken broth. Bring 2 litres of water to the boil in a stockpot or large saucepan. Add the chicken bones, spring onion whites and celery. Reduce the heat to medium-low and simmer for 1 hour. Strain into a clean pan, then add salt and pepper to taste.

While the broth is simmering, blanch the pak choi by pouring just-boiled water over them and draining straight away.

Next, make the chicken oil. Heat the groundnut oil in a large frying pan on a high heat, add the chicken skin pieces and fry for 5–6 minutes until crisp. Reduce the heat to low, add the other chicken oil ingredients and fry for a further 10 minutes. Discard the garlic and ginger, and eat the chicken skin (chef's perk!). Pour the chicken oil into a small bowl and set to one side. (Don't wash the frying pan yet.)

Grind the spice paste ingredients, except the oil, in a blender or food processor until smooth. Heat the oil on a high heat in the frying pan you used to make the chicken oil. Add the spice paste and fry for 2–3 minutes until fragrant. Add the diced chicken meat and fry for 5–6 minutes until the chicken is cooked.

Cook the noodles according to packet instructions; drain, then dress with the light soy sauce, sweet soy sauce, Worcestershire sauce and salt and pepper to taste. Divide among 4 noodle bowls, garnish with the diced chicken and drizzle each serving with 2 tablespoons chicken oil.

Bring the chicken broth back to the boil. Add the pak choi and 1–2 ladles of simmering chicken broth to each bowl. Garnish the bowls with fried dumpling skins, spring onion greens, celery leaves and fried shallots. Serve immediately, with chopsticks and Chinese spoons. Pour the rest of the chicken broth into 4 small soup bowls and serve on the side along with the chilli garlic sauce.

Cook's Tip
Any leftover chicken oil can be kept in an airtight container for up to a week – drizzle it on noodles, pasta and even rice to give a savoury kick.

Ribbon Noodles with Scrambled Egg Sauce

Wat Tan Hor (Malaysia)

This is the Malay saucy sister to the Thai/Lao dish *Rad Na*. The main difference is that *Wat Tan Hor* is topped with a swirl of scrambled egg, which makes the dish even silkier and richer.

Serves 4 | Takes 30 minutes to make, 16 minutes to cook

400g fresh broad, flat rice noodles (*ho fun*) or 150g dried
2 skinless, boneless chicken thighs, about 200g total weight, cut into small strips
2 tbsp groundnut oil
1 tbsp dark soy sauce
4 cloves garlic, finely chopped
100g ready-made fish balls, halved
12 raw king prawns, peeled and deveined
200g choy sum, chopped
Fried Shallots (Secret Weapons, page 11)
1 tsp toasted sesame oil

For the chicken marinade
1 tsp cornflour
1 tsp Chinese rice wine or dry sherry
1 tsp light soy sauce
1 tsp dark soy sauce
1 tsp caster sugar
1 tsp toasted sesame oil
pinch each of salt and pepper

For the scrambled egg sauce
750ml chicken or vegetable stock
1 tbsp Chinese rice wine or dry sherry
1 tbsp oyster sauce
1 tbsp light soy sauce
1 tbsp caster sugar
3 tbsp cornflour mixed with 6 tbsp cold water
salt and pepper to taste
2 eggs, beaten

If using fresh *ho fun*, carefully separate the noodles (they should come apart in 2.5cm strands) and set them aside, lightly covered with a damp cloth or clingfilm. If using dried *ho fun*, put them in a large heatproof bowl and generously cover with just-boiled water. After a minute, untangle the noodles, then leave them to soak for a further 6 minutes until al dente. Drain in a colander and rinse thoroughly under running cold water. Set to one side in the colander so that any residual water can continue to drain.

Mix together the ingredients for the chicken marinade in a bowl. Add the chicken and toss to coat, then leave to marinate for 15 minutes.

Heat 1 tablespoon oil in a wok or deep frying pan on a medium heat. Add the noodles and dark soy sauce. Stir-fry for 2–3 minutes until the noodles have absorbed the colour of the soy and turned brown. Remove and keep warm on a serving dish or platter.

Heat the remaining oil in the wok on a high heat, then stir-fry the garlic for 1–2 minutes until fragrant. Add the chicken and stir-fry for 2–3 minutes until it changes colour.

Now add the stock, rice wine, oyster sauce, light soy sauce and sugar. Bring to the boil, then add the fish balls, prawns and choy sum. Cook for a further 2–3 minutes. Turn the heat down to medium, then add the cornflour mix to the wok and stir to combine. Season to taste with salt and pepper. Simmer for 5 minutes until the sauce has thickened.

Remove the wok from the heat and drizzle the beaten eggs into the sauce. Stir so the egg cooks lightly. Pour the finished egg sauce over the warm noodles. Sprinkle with fried shallots and drizzle with sesame oil. Give everyone a noodle bowl and chopsticks to help themselves and serve immediately.

Soft Tofu and Kimchi Noodles

Sundubu Jjigae (Korea)

A double whammy of chilli heat and steaming broth is guaranteed to keep the chills away, and one of my weapons of choice is the Korean dish *Sundubu Jjigae*. It's a hot and spicy stew made with super-soft uncurdled tofu, seafood, mushrooms, onions, kelp and *gochujang* (a Korean chilli paste). A raw egg is cracked straight into the stew just before it's time to eat. The combination of barely poached egg and cloud-like tofu dancing together in the intense broth is obscenely good, especially when you break into the egg and the soft golden yolk melds with it all. *Sundubu Jjigae* should really be cooked and served in special bowls and eaten with rice, but I often just use a saucepan and chuck it over noodles for a quick and lazy meal.

Serves 2 | Takes 15 minutes to make, 25 minutes to cook

300g fresh udon noodles (**yude udon**)
1 sachet of instant dashi or 10g kombu flakes
6 fresh shiitake mushrooms, sliced
6 cloves garlic, peeled
1 white onion, quartered
8 dried anchovies (**ikan bilis**), heads removed
2 tbsp groundnut oil
2 tbsp Korean pepper paste (**gochujang**)
2 handfuls of small clams in the shell or peeled large raw prawns, deveined
1 packet of extra-soft tofu (**sundubu**)
2 spring onions (green and white parts), shredded
1 fresh red finger chilli, sliced
2 eggs
Korean fermented pickle (**kimchi**), to serve

Blanch the noodles by pouring just-boiled water over them in a bowl and leaving them for 5 minutes, then drain. Divide between 2 noodle bowls.

Put the dashi or kombu flakes, mushrooms, garlic, onion and anchovies in a saucepan and add 500ml cold water. Bring to a vigorous boil, then reduce the heat and simmer for 15 minutes to make your *jjigae* stock. Pour into a bowl and set to one side.

Add the oil and Korean pepper paste to the saucepan. Heat on a high heat for 2–3 minutes until sizzling. Pour the stock back into the saucepan (don't bother straining the stock – the softened garlic, mushrooms and onion are part of the stew). Top up with water if necessary (different brands of instant dashi are saltier than others, and different brands of Korean pepper paste can be spicier than others), then bring to the boil.

Add the clams or prawns to the saucepan, and bring to the boil again. Add the extra-soft tofu and gently break it up into clumps. Bring the stew to the boil one more time, then crack in the eggs so they can poach gently.

Ladle the stew into the noodle bowls, making sure each bowl has an egg. Top with kimchi, spring onions and chilli and serve immediately, with chopsticks and tablespoons.

Turmeric Fish and Dill

Chả Cá Lã Vọng (Vietnam)

Chả Cá Lã Vọng (or, to give it its proper name, *Chả Cá Thăng Long*) is an infamous dish from Hanoi in Vietnam, beloved by rock and roll chefs such as Anthony Bourdain for the theatrical way in which it's served. It's the only dish on the menu at the legendary Chả Cá Lã Vọng restaurant – fillets of fish (traditionally basa river catfish) are marinated in turmeric, then fried and sizzled table-side, flames a-leaping, with lots of fresh dill. The fragrance is incredible as the herbs and spices fill the air, and each mouthful is a riot of flavours and textures.

Serves 4 | Takes 1 hour 20 minutes to make, 8 minutes to cook

500g fillets from a firm white fish such as haddock, cod or pollock, cut into 5cm wide pieces
300g dried thick, round rice noodles (Vietnamese *bún*)
plain flour, for dusting
6 tbsp groundnut oil
3 cloves garlic, crushed
8 spring onions, cut into 4cm segments and white parts split lengthways
2 large handfuls of fresh dill fronds, coarsely chopped

For the fish marinade
4 tbsp groundnut oil
1 tbsp fresh dill fronds
3cm knob of fresh turmeric root, peeled, or 1 tbsp ground turmeric
1cm piece of fresh galangal, peeled
1cm piece of fresh root ginger, peeled
1 tbsp Vietnamese fine shrimp paste (*mắm ruốc*)
1 tbsp caster sugar
1 tbsp fish sauce
1 tsp freshly ground black pepper
1/2 tsp salt

For the dipping sauce
1 tbsp Vietnamese fine shrimp paste (*mắm ruốc*)
2 cloves garlic, finely chopped
1 fresh red finger chilli, finely chopped
juice of 2 limes
1 tbsp caster sugar
1 tbsp hot water

To serve
handful of salted peanuts, crushed
sprigs of fresh coriander, mint and Thai basil, plus (if possible) Vietnamese balm (*kinh giới*) and Vietnamese coriander (laksa leaf/*rau răm*)

Blitz the fish marinade ingredients together in a blender or food processor until they form a smooth paste. Tip into a bowl, add the fish and turn to coat. Cover and leave to marinate in the fridge for 1 hour.

Meanwhile, put the noodles in a large heatproof bowl and generously cover with just-boiled water. Leave to soak for 1 hour. Drain in a colander and rinse thoroughly with running cold water, then set to one side in the colander so that any residual water can continue to drain.

Whisk together the ingredients for the dipping sauce. Set aside to mellow.

Take the fish out of the fridge and drain off the marinade. Pat the fish pieces dry with kitchen paper, then dust with a little plain flour.

You will want to eat as soon as the fish is cooked, so reheat the noodles now by placing the colander in your sink and pouring a kettleful of boiling water over them. Divide the noodles among 4 bowls. Have the peanuts and dipping sauce in bowls on the table.

Put the oil and garlic in a cast-iron pan, fajita pan or wok (see Cook's Tip). Heat it on a medium-high heat, then add the fish. Cook for 3–4 minutes, then flip over and cook for a further 2 minutes. Turn the heat up to high, add the spring onion white parts and the dill, and sauté for 1–2 minutes longer. By now, both sides of the fish pieces should be golden with a slight crust.

Bring the sizzling pan to the table. Tell everyone to grab a bowl, then top their noodles with the fish and dill, drizzle over plenty of dipping sauce and scatter on some crushed peanuts and herb sprigs. Mix well and eat with chopsticks.

Cook's Tip
Part of the joy of this dish is the theatre of having it cooked right in front of you. So ideally you'd do this in a tabletop cooker.

Mogok Round Rice Noodles

Mogok Meeshay (Burma)

As I said before, my mother's family is from Mogok in Burma. It's a gem-mining town, remarkable for the fact that it's where ninety per cent of the world's rubies come from. In fact, my great, great-grandfather was U Hmat, known as the Ruby King of Burma, who famously traded in precious gemstones in the late 1800s and was rumoured to have been knighted by Queen Victoria in absentia. Sadly, the family money has long since gone, but never mind rubies – in Mogok, pork is king and every little bit is used, from head to tail. So valued is this meat in my mother's birthplace that the Mogok slang for wages is *we(t)-thar bo* – literally 'pork funds' – and people would say cheerily, 'I'm off to earn today's pork funds now' (compare 'bringing home the bacon'). This Mogok dish of rice noodles and pork is an absolute favourite of mine. I make it at least once a week and I request it from my mother whenever I visit her.

Serves 4 | Takes 1 hour to make, 3 hours to cook

300g dried thick, round rice noodles (Vietnamese *bún* or Guilin rice vermicelli)

For the broth
1 x 1kg piece of pork belly
1/2 tsp MSG or 2 tbsp Marigold bouillon powder
1 tbsp caster sugar
1/2 tsp salt

For the condiments
Burmese Rice Sauce (*gaw-yay*), (Secret Weapons, page 10)
4 tbsp Tamarind Juice (Secret Weapons, page 13)
2 tbsp caster sugar
50ml malt vinegar
1 tsp salt
1/4 bunch of fresh coriander, stems very finely chopped and leaves chopped
light soy sauce
dark soy sauce

For the garnish
Fried Shallots (Secret Weapons, page 11)
Crispy Garlic Oil (Secret Weapons, page 11)
Chilli Oil (Secret Weapons, page 11)

Put the noodles in a large heatproof bowl and generously cover with just-boiled water. Leave to soak for 1 hour. Drain in a colander and rinse thoroughly with running cold water, then set to one side in the colander so that any residual water can continue to drain.

Now make the broth. Put the pork belly, MSG and sugar in a medium saucepan with 1 litre water. Bring to the boil, then reduce the heat to medium-low and simmer for 3 hours, skimming any scum from the surface.

Lift out the pork, which should be as tender as anything by now, and place it in a small saucepan. Roughly snip into small chunks with kitchen scissors. Add a ladle of the pork broth to moisten and stir this pork sauce, then set to one side. Keep the broth and the pork sauce warm.

Make the Burmese rice sauce, then add the tamarind juice, sugar, vinegar and salt and mix thoroughly. Simmer for 30 minutes on a medium-low heat.

Put the coriander stems in a small bowl and add 100ml water and a pinch of salt. Mix well, then add the coriander leaves and stir gently.

When you're ready to serve, reheat the noodles by placing the colander in your sink and pouring a kettleful of boiling water over them. Divide the noodles among 4 noodle bowls.

To each bowl, add 3 tablespoons tamarind rice sauce, 3 tablespoons pork sauce and 1 ladleful of pork broth. Now add 1 tablespoon light soy sauce and 1 teaspoon dark soy sauce to each bowl. Lastly add 1 tablespoon coriander 'salsa' to each bowl, sprinkle some fried shallots on top and drizzle over 1 tablespoon garlic oil.

Heat the remaining broth until simmering, then divide among 4 small soup bowls. Add 1 teaspoon coriander 'salsa' to each bowl.

Serve the noodles immediately, with chopsticks and Chinese spoons, along with the chilli oil for people to help themselves and the bowls of pork broth on the side.

Shan Noodles

Shan Khao Swè (Burma)

Here, from the Shan State in Burma, is another of what I consider to be my heritage recipes – I worked out recently that I'm around 40 per cent Shan and 10 per cent Intha, the latter being the people from Inle Lake, famous for its leg-rowers and also of Shan derivation. Some people like their noodles rich with plenty of tomatoes (like I do) while others prefer a clearer broth, but the important thing about this dish is that it should be sweet but smoky, and warm you from the inside-out.

Serves 4 | Takes 15 minutes to make, 40 minutes to cook

400g dried narrow, flat rice noodles (*bánh phở*, if possible)
small bunch of spring onions
2 cloves garlic, peeled
4 fresh ripe tomatoes or ½ tin plum tomatoes
4 tbsp groundnut oil
handful of dried shrimps
400g minced chicken (preferably thigh meat)
1 tbsp freshly ground black pepper
1 tbsp fish sauce
1 tsp caster sugar
1 tbsp sweet paprika
1 tsp hot chilli powder

To serve
preserved mustard greens, chopped
Cabbage and Cucumber Salad (Secret Weapons, page 11)
Chilli Oil (Secret Weapons, page 11)
handful of fresh coriander leaves, shredded

Put the noodles in a large heatproof bowl and generously cover with just-boiled water. After a minute, untangle the noodles, then leave them to soak for a further 8 minutes. Drain in a colander and rinse thoroughly under running cold water. Set to one side in the colander so that any residual water can continue to drain.

Cut off the spring onion bulbs and put them in a blender or food processor (thinly slice the green parts and keep for later). Add the garlic and tomatoes to the blender and blitz to a smooth purée. Heat 2 tablespoons oil in a deep saucepan on a high heat and sauté the purée for 5 minutes until it stops smelling raw. Set to one side.

Toast the dried shrimps by tossing them in a dry frying pan on a high heat for 5 minutes until charred and smelling smoky. Turn the heat down to medium and add the remaining oil and the chicken mince. Fry for a further 10 minutes until the chicken is browned, breaking it up with a spoon.

Add the chicken and shrimp mix to the saucepan of purée along with the pepper, fish sauce, sugar, paprika and chilli powder plus 1 litre of water. Stir well. Bring to the boil, then simmer for 20 minutes.

When you're ready to serve, reheat the noodles by placing the colander in your sink and pouring a kettleful of boiling water over them. Divide the noodles between 2 noodle bowls and add a generous ladleful of the chicken sauce to each bowl. Top with mustard greens, cabbage salad, chilli oil, spring onion greens and shredded coriander leaves. Serve immediately, with chopsticks and Chinese spoons.

Cook's Tip
Some people add crushed peanuts as a garnish, which gives a good crunch. Chinese vendors in Burma have been known to add five spice powder, but this overwhelms what is quite a delicate dish so I'd avoid.

Mandalay Round Rice Noodles

Mandalay Meeshay (Burma)

In this glorious dish, thick, round rice noodles are doused in a sour, sweet, savoury, salty, garlicky mix. Mandalay is famous for its *lun-bay zah* – literally 'roadside fare', or street food. Every day, my 6ft 4in grandfather 'Po Po' would sit in his huge wicker chair at the side of the house so he could watch life go by and flag down every passing snack-seller. I had him on special alert for the Mandalay *meeshay* seller who'd trot past with his wares hanging off a pole on his shoulder. This is my favourite Burmese dish – not just in noodle terms. I've given you the recipe for the luxury version, which uses chicken. The everyday version uses the pork sauce you find with Mogok Round Rice Noodles – that, and the type of noodle, is why they're both called *meeshay*. (*Meeshay* in turn is a corruption of the Chinese *mĭxiàn* – they're the same type of noodle.)

Serves 4–6 | Takes 1 hour to make, 2 hours 20 minutes to cook

300g dried thick, round rice noodles (Vietnamese *bún* or Guilin rice vermicelli)

For the chicken broth and sauce
500g skinless chicken thighs (on the bone)
1/4 bunch fresh coriander, stems very finely chopped to a paste and leaves chopped
2 cloves garlic, peeled
1/2 tsp MSG or 2 tbsp Marigold bouillon powder
1 tsp caster sugar
3 tbsp groundnut oil
3 medium onions, chopped
2 tbsp sweet paprika
1 tsp hot chilli powder

For the crispy omelette
1 heaped tbsp self-raising flour
2 tbsp cold water
2 eggs
1/2 tsp salt
7 tbsp groundnut oil

For the condiments
8 cloves garlic, peeled
Burmese Rice Sauce (Secret Weapons, page 10)
Burmese Water Pickle (Secret Weapons, page 10)
Chinese black vinegar
yellow soybean sauce
light soy sauce
freshly ground black pepper

For the garnish
beansprouts, topped and tailed and blanched
Fried Shallots (Secret Weapons, page 11)
Chilli Oil (Secret Weapons, page 11)

Put the noodles in a large heatproof bowl and generously cover with just-boiled water. Leave to soak for 1 hour. Drain in a colander and rinse thoroughly with running cold water, then set to one side in the colander so that any residual water can continue to drain.

Now make the broth. Put the chicken, the finely chopped coriander stems, garlic, half of the MSG or bouillon powder and the sugar into a medium saucepan with 1 litre of water. Bring to the boil, then reduce the heat to medium-low and simmer for 1 hour, skimming any scum from the surface. Remove the chicken, take the meat off the bone and pull it into large strips; set to one side. Keep the chicken broth warm.

Heat the oil in another medium saucepan on a high heat. Add the onions and stir-fry for 3 minutes until fragrant. Reduce the heat to medium-low and add 100ml water, the remaining MSG or bouillon powder, the paprika and chilli powder. Mix thoroughly, then leave to sweat gently, stirring occasionally, for 1–2 hours until the onions have broken down completely. If it looks like the onions might stick and burn at any point, add a little water and continue cooking and stirring. Now add a ladleful of the chicken broth and stir well before adding the chicken meat. Set this chicken sauce to one side but keep warm.

Make the crispy omelette next. Combine all the ingredients, except the oil, in a bowl and whisk to make a smooth batter. Pour the oil into a wok or large frying pan and heat on a high heat. When you can feel waves of heat rising from the oil with the palm of your hand, swirl the oil around, then pour the batter evenly on to the wok or pan; the batter will puff up almost immediately to form a large cloud. Leave for 30 seconds before using a spatula to 'chop' the cloud into big fluffy pieces. After 1 minute, flip each piece gently to ensure an even colour on both sides. When the omelette pieces are crisp and golden brown, scoop them out with a slotted spoon and drain on kitchen paper. Pour the oil you've used for frying (known in Burmese as 'hsi-jet', which literally means 'cooked oil') into a small bowl and reserve for dressing the noodles later.

For the coriander and garlic condiment, pound the garlic in a pestle and mortar until it is a rough purée. Transfer to a small bowl.

Add 50ml water and mix well, then add the chopped coriander leaves and stir in gently.

When you're ready to serve, reheat the noodles by placing the colander in your sink and pouring a kettleful of boiling water over them. Divide the noodles among 4 noodle bowls.

To each bowl, add 2 tablespoons Burmese rice sauce, 3 tablespoons chicken sauce and 1 tablespoon of the 'cooked' oil. Now add 1 tablespoon water pickle, 1 tablespoon vinegar, 1 teaspoon soybean sauce and 1 teaspoon light soy sauce. Lastly add 1 tablespoon coriander and garlic condiment, some fried shallots and some beansprouts.

Bring the chicken broth back to a simmer, then pour into 4 small soup bowls. Add 1 teaspoon coriander and garlic condiment, $1/2$ teaspoon soybean sauce and some freshly ground black pepper to each bowl.

Serve the noodles immediately, with chopsticks and Chinese spoons, with the chilli oil for people to help themselves and the bowls of chicken broth on the side.

Rakhine Fish Noodles

Yakhine Mohntee/Ar-Pu Shar-Pu (Burma)

This peppery fish dish, from the Rakhine people in Burma, is often compared to *Mohinga* (page 74). It's a much thinner broth, however, and the main note is provided by galangal, whereas *Mohinga* relies on lemongrass for its vegetal hit. This also uses shrimp paste, known as *ngapi* in Burmese – it's said that if you don't like *ngapi* then you will never understand Burma. Some people prefer *Yakhine Mohntee* as a sort of salad, with the noodles mixed with all the garnishes and the broth served on the side. Its other name, *Ar-pu Shar-pu*, is a joke derived from its peppery nature – it literally means 'mouth burns, tongue burns'. This is usually made with small river catfish known in Burmese as *nga gyi*, *nga ku* and *nga yunt*. Fresh tilapia or grey mullet have a similar texture and flavour.

Serves 4 | Takes 30 minutes to make, 1 hour 30 minutes to cook

300g dried rice vermicelli noodles
1 tsp black peppercorns
4 cloves garlic (skin on)
3 tbsp shrimp paste (*ngapi*)
3cm knob of fresh galangal, about 80g, smashed (skin on)
10 fresh red finger chillies, destalked
pinch of salt
500g fresh tilapia or mullet fillets, skinned
$\frac{1}{4}$ tsp MSG or 1 tbsp Marigold bouillon powder
1 tbsp fish sauce
$\frac{1}{4}$ tsp ground turmeric
4 tbsp groundnut oil
salt and freshly ground black pepper

To serve

200g ready-made fishcake, sliced
Tamarind Juice (Secret Weapons, page 13)
Crispy Garlic Oil (Secret Weapons, page 11)
Yellow Split-pea Crackers (Secret Weapons, page 13)
large handful of fresh coriander leaves, chopped
fish sauce

Put the noodles into a heatproof bowl, generously cover with just-boiled water and untangle with a fork, then leave to soak for 15 minutes. Drain in a colander and rinse with cold water, then set to one side in the colander so the noodles can continue to drain.

Pound the peppercorns with the garlic in a pestle and mortar to make a coarse paste. Set to one side.

Bring 1.5 litres water to the boil in a stockpot or large saucepan. Add the peppercorn and garlic paste, the shrimp paste and the smashed galangal. Turn the heat down to medium and simmer the broth for 1 hour.

Meanwhile, put the chillies in a small saucepan, cover with water and bring to the boil, then turn the heat down to medium and simmer for 15 minutes. Spoon 4 tablespoons of the cooking liquid into a small bowl, then drain the chillies. Pound them with a pinch of salt in a pestle and mortar to a paste. Add to the reserved liquid in the bowl and mix to make a sauce. Set aside.

Bring the stockpot of broth back to the boil. Add the fish, then turn the heat down to medium and simmer for 5 minutes until the fish is cooked. Remove the fish with a fish slice. Strain the broth into a clean pan, discarding the solids.

Flake half the fish fillets and add to the strained broth along with the MSG, fish sauce, a pinch of salt and pepper to taste. Take the rest of the fish between your palms and gently squeeze out the liquid into the strained broth. Pat the fish dry with kitchen paper, dust with the turmeric and set to one side.

Heat 2 tablespoons oil in a frying pan on medium heat. Add the fishcake and fry for 5 minutes until cooked. Remove from the pan and set to one side.

Heat the remaining oil in the pan. Add the turmeric-dusted fish pieces and fry on medium heat for 3 minutes on each side until golden brown. Flake the fried fish and place in a dish.

When you're ready to serve, bring the broth back to the boil. Divide the noodles among 4 pasta dishes and top with the flaked fried fish, tamarind juice, the chilli sauce you made earlier, garlic oil, split-pea crackers and coriander.

Now you can either mix everything together and eat the noodles as a salad, with the broth served in a separate bowl on the side, or you can pour the broth over everything. Whichever method you choose, serve with spoons and forks or Chinese spoons.

Salted Soybean Ribbon Noodles

Hsan Khao Swè (Burma)

This Burmese dish is a weeknight standby for me – I grab dried noodles from the cupboard and whatever protein there is to hand in the fridge. The yellow soybean sauce provides a deeply savoury, salty hit that helps pep me up for the rest of the week. Incidentally, *Hsan Khao Swè* literally means 'rice noodles' in Burmese, but it's always taken to mean broad, flat rice or ribbon noodles.

Serves 2 | Takes 15 minutes to make, 5 minutes to cook

150g dried broad, flat rice noodles (*ho fun*)
200g beansprouts, topped and tailed
150g any cooked meat or tofu, sliced
2 tsp yellow soybean sauce
2 tbsp dark soy sauce
2 tbsp light soy sauce
4 tbsp preserved mustard greens, chopped
750ml vegetable or meat stock
$1/4$ tsp MSG or 1 tbsp Marigold bouillon powder
1 tsp caster sugar

To serve
handful of fresh coriander leaves, chopped
2 spring onions (green and white parts), finely sliced
Fried Shallots (Secret Weapons, page 11)
Chilli Oil (Secret Weapons, page 11)

Put the noodles in a large heatproof bowl and generously cover with just-boiled water. After a minute, untangle the noodles, then leave them to soak for a further 8 minutes. Drain in a colander and rinse thoroughly under running cold water. Set to one side in the colander so that any residual water can continue to drain.

Blanch the beansprouts by pouring just-boiled water over them and then draining straight away.

When you're ready to serve, divide the noodles between 2 noodle bowls. Top each bowl with half of the sliced meat/tofu, yellow soybean sauce, dark and light soy sauces, preserved mustard greens and beansprouts.

Bring the stock to a rolling boil with the MSG and sugar in a saucepan, then ladle over each bowl of noodles. Sprinkle with the coriander, spring onions and fried shallots. Serve with chopsticks and Chinese spoons, and chilli oil on the side.

Saucy Chicken and Peanut Noodles

Gaw-yay Khao Swè (Burma)

A dish popular in Upper Burma, this is notable for its deliciously rich sauce, which makes the noodles slip down into your belly with frightening ease. I spent ages trying to think of a good translation for the title as *gaw-yay* literally means 'glue water' (in this case, it's made from tapioca, so you can see my double dilemma). Anyway, that's why I called it Saucy Chicken and Peanut Noodles, although you can use pork fillet (tenderloin) as well, or even tofu. The sauce is the thing.

Serves 2 | Takes 25 minutes to make, 50 minutes to cook

150g dried standard thick wheat noodles (*lo mein*)
2 cloves garlic, peeled
1 tbsp caster sugar
1 tsp salt
2 skinless, boneless chicken thighs, about 200g total weight, diced
3 tbsp groundnut oil
1 medium onion, chopped
1 heaped tbsp tapioca flour mixed with enough cold water to form a gluey paste
$1/4$ tsp MSG or 1 tbsp Marigold bouillon powder

To serve

Cabbage and Cucumber Salad (Secret Weapons, page 11)
Fried Shallots (Secret Weapons, page 11)
Fried Peanuts (Secret Weapons, page 11)
4 spring onions (green and white parts), thinly sliced
handful of fresh coriander leaves, chopped
Chilli Oil (Secret Weapons, page 11)
freshly ground black pepper

Cook the noodles according to the packet instructions. Drain in a colander and rinse thoroughly with cold water, then set to one side in the colander so that any residual water can continue to drain.

Bring 1 litre water to the boil in a medium saucepan. Add the garlic, sugar, salt and chicken. Turn the heat down to medium-low, cover with a lid and leave to simmer gently for 20 minutes.

Meanwhile, heat the oil in a wok or deep frying pan on a medium heat and fry the onion for 5–6 minutes until translucent. Add the tapioca paste and MSG and whisk to combine. Now add the poached chicken with a ladleful of the poaching liquid (reserve the rest of the liquid to serve on the side). Stir everything in the wok to combine and then simmer for a further 10 minutes.

Reheat the noodles by placing the colander in your sink and pouring a kettleful of boiling water over them. Divide the noodles among 4 noodle bowls and top each with a generous ladleful of the chicken and tapioca sauce.

Garnish with the cabbage salad, fried shallots and peanuts, spring onions, half of the coriander and some chilli oil, then serve with chopsticks. Serve the poaching liquid in small soup bowls with Chinese spoons on the side, sprinkled with the rest of the coriander and some black pepper.

Pork, Tomato, Kaffir Lime and Celery Noodles
(fusion)

I was convinced this was a Burmese dish until my mother disabused me of the notion and told me I'd made it up. It has recognisable Burmese elements though, which is my excuse. I guess it's an Asian spag bol – just as comforting but with added spice and zing.

Serves 4 | Takes 10 minutes to make, 1 hour 15 minutes to cook

1 bunch of fresh celery, with plenty of leaves
2 tbsp groundnut oil
1 medium onion, finely chopped
400g minced pork
1x 400g tin chopped plum tomatoes
1 tbsp ground dried kaffir lime leaves
1 tbsp hot paprika
1 tsp mild chilli powder
2 tbsp fish sauce
400g spaghetti
4 spring onions (green and white parts), thinly sliced
2 fresh red finger chillies, sliced into rings

To serve
lime wedges
fish sauce

Remove the celery leaves, chop roughly and set to one side. Chop the celery sticks into 2.5cm pieces, discarding any stringy or woody parts.

Heat the oil in a large saucepan and fry the onion for 5 minutes on a high heat until translucent. Add the celery pieces and fry for another 5 minutes. Add the minced pork and fry for 5 minutes until the meat browns, breaking it up with a spoon.

Now add the tomatoes, kaffir lime powder, paprika, chilli powder, fish sauce and 1 litre of just-boiled water. Bring to the boil, then reduce the heat and simmer, uncovered, for 1 hour until the tomatoes, celery and onions break down and reduce into a thick sauce. (You can freeze the sauce now for up to a month.)

Cook the spaghetti in a large pot of boiling salted water according to packet directions. Drain in a colander, then rinse with cold water to stop the cooking process. (Unlike in Western pasta dishes, the spaghetti is rinsed to get rid of excess starch.) Set to one side in the colander.

When you're ready to serve, reheat the spaghetti by pouring a kettleful of boiling water over it. Divide among 4 pasta dishes and ladle a generous amount of sauce on to each. Top with the celery leaves, spring onions and chillies. Serve immediately with spoons and forks, and lime wedges and fish sauce on the side.

SALADS

Grilled Pork Patties and Herbs

Bún Chả (Vietnam)

This Vietnamese dish is thought to have originated from Hanoi. Made of char-grilled fatty pork (*chả*) served over round rice noodles (*bún*), the sweet smokiness of the dish is so compelling that in 1959 Vietnamese food writer Vu Bang described Hanoi as a town 'transfixed by *bún chả*'.

Serves 4 | Takes 2 hours
40 minutes to make,
20 minutes to cook

300g dried rice vermicelli noodles

For the pork patties
2 tbsp palm sugar or soft dark brown sugar
500g minced pork with plenty of fat
1 large shallot, finely chopped
2 cloves garlic, finely chopped
2 tbsp fish sauce
1 tsp freshly ground black pepper
1/2 tsp salt

For the pickled vegetables
1 medium carrot, cut into thin half-moons
200g fresh white radish (mooli/daikon), peeled and cut into thin half-moons
1 tbsp golden caster sugar
pinch of salt
100ml rice vinegar

For the warm dipping sauce
50ml fish sauce
50ml rice vinegar
2 tbsp golden caster sugar
1 fresh red finger chilli, chopped
2 cloves garlic, chopped
juice of 1/2 lime

To serve
1 cos lettuce, shredded
sprigs of fresh mint
sprigs of fresh coriander
large handful of purple shiso leaves

First make the pork patties. Heat the sugar with 75ml water in a small saucepan on a high heat. Whisk and heat for 6–7 minutes until a dark brown caramel forms. Remove from the heat and add 50ml cold water, swirling the saucepan so the water mixes with the caramel. Pour the caramel sauce into a bowl and leave to cool.

Add the remaining ingredients for the pork patties to the bowl and mix well. Cover and leave to marinate in the fridge for 2 hours.

Meanwhile, make the pickled vegetables. Put the carrot and white radish in a shallow bowl, sprinkle with the sugar and salt, and rub into the vegetables. Pour over the vinegar. Leave to pickle for at least 15 minutes.

Put the noodles into a heatproof bowl, generously cover with just-boiled water and untangle with a fork, then leave to soak for 15 minutes. Drain in a colander and rinse with cold water. Set to one side in the colander to drain thoroughly.

Take the pork mix from the fridge. Oil your hands, then form the pork into ping-pong balls. Gently press down on each ball to make a small patty or mini-burger. Set to one side.

Now prepare your barbecue or table-top charcoal grill, or preheat your grill to medium-high.

Next, make the dipping sauce. Combine the fish sauce, vinegar, sugar and 100ml water in a saucepan. Mix well, then bring to the boil. Remove from the heat and keep warm.

When the barbecue or grill are ready for cooking, grill the patties for 4–5 minutes on each side.

Meanwhile, pour the dipping sauce into 4 small bowls. Add the chilli, garlic and lime juice to each and stir.

Divide the noodles among 4 pasta bowls and top with the pork patties, lettuce, pickled vegetables and fresh herbs. Serve with the warm sauce on the side. Tell diners they can either pour the sauce all over their bowls and dig in, or they can dip and eat mouthfuls as they go.

Ramen Salad – Hiyashi Chūka

(Japan)

Hiyashi Chūka is a classic summer dish in Japan consisting of chilled ramen noodles with various toppings. It's bright and colourful with lots of crunch – guaranteed to cool you down in a heatwave.

Serves 2 | Takes 30 minutes to make, 15 minutes to cook

200g fresh ramen noodles (*chūkamen*)

For the dressing
2 tbsp sesame seeds or 1 tbsp Chinese sesame paste or tahini
1cm piece of fresh root ginger, peeled
3 tbsp rice vinegar
3 tbsp Japanese soy sauce (*shoyu*)
3 tbsp chicken stock or Dashi (page 9)
2 tbsp caster sugar
2 tbsp toasted sesame oil
1 tbsp Japanese mustard (*karashi*), or 1 tsp English mustard made up from powder

For the sweet omelette crêpe (*kinshi tamago*)
2 eggs
1 tbsp sake
1 tbsp Dashi (page 9)
1 tsp caster sugar
1/2 tsp salt
groundnut oil

For the toppings
1/2 Asian or Lebanese cucumber or 1/4 regular cucumber, peeled, deseeded and julienned
150g cooked ham, sliced into matchsticks
1 tomato, deseeded and cut into thin wedges

For the garnish
2 spring onions (green and white parts), shredded
dried nori seaweed strips
sesame seeds
Japanese red pickled ginger (*beni shoga*)
Japanese mustard (*karashi*)

First make the dressing. If using sesame seeds, grind them to a powder in a pestle and mortar. Put the ground sesame (or tahini) in a bowl or jug. Now pound the ginger in the pestle and mortar to a pulp (or you can grate the ginger, then add 2 tablespoons hot water and mix). Squeeze the ginger in your hand over the bowl containing the sesame, so the ginger juice runs in; discard the pulp. Add all the other dressing ingredients to the bowl and whisk thoroughly. Keep in the fridge until needed.

Next, make the omelette crêpes. Lightly whisk the eggs with the sake, dashi, sugar and salt. Heat 1 tablespoon oil in a frying pan on a medium-high heat for a minute, then swirl the pan so the bottom is covered with oil. Remove from the heat and pour in some of the egg mixture. Swirl the pan again so the egg spreads out and cooks to a thin omelette in the residual heat. Flip over (don't let it brown), then transfer to a plate and leave to cool. Repeat to make 3 or 4 more crêpes. When they are cool, roll them up on a chopping board and cut across into thin slices with a sharp knife. Wrap in clingfilm and set to one side.

Cook the noodles according to the packet instruction. Drain and rinse with plenty of cold water, then chill in a bowl of iced water.

When you're ready to serve, drain the noodles thoroughly and divide between 2 pasta dishes. Lay the omelette strips, cucumber, ham and tomato on the noodles one after another so they radiate from the middle in a sunburst pattern. Drizzle the chilled dressing over the top. Scatter with the spring onions, nori strips and sesame seeds, and serve with the pickled ginger and mustard on the side.

Cook's Tip
The toppings here are traditional for ramen salad, but you'll also find it served with cooked chicken or pork, blanched beansprouts and carrots, sweetcorn, wakame seaweed, cooked prawns and even crabsticks. The world's your oyster.

Chilled Udon with Splashed Sauce

Bukkake Udon (Japan)

This chilled dish of *udon* noodles, with various toppings providing different flavours and textures, is splashed with a strong sweet and salty sauce (the verb *bukkakeru* means 'to splash, pour or throw on'). It's a speciality of the city of Kurashiki in the Okayama prefecture in Japan.

Serves 2 | Takes 30 minutes to make, 10 minutes to cook

200g dried udon noodles (*udon*) or 300g fresh (*yude udon*)
bonito flakes (*katsuobushi*)

For the sauce (*mentsuyu*)
4 tbsp mirin
4 tbsp Japanese soy sauce (*shoyu*)
250ml Dashi (page 9)
1 tsp caster sugar

For the toppings (choose one from each section below or any combination you like)

Egg
Hot Spring Eggs (Secret Weapons, page 12)
raw egg yolk or whole quail's egg
Fresh greens
2 spring onions (green and white parts), shredded
fresh shiso leaves, thinly sliced
Seaweed
dried nori seaweed strips
rehydrated wakame seaweed pieces

For tartness
grated white radish (daikon/mooli)
grated fresh root ginger
For crunch
Tempura Crumbs (*tenkasu*), (Secret Weapons, page 13)
sesame seeds
For saltiness
Japanese fermented soybeans (*natto*)
salt-pickled Japanese apricot (*umeboshi*)
For heat
wasabi paste
shichimi pepper (*shichimi togarashi*)

If using dried *udon*, bring a medium saucepan half full of water to the boil. Scatter the noodles into the water, then immediately reduce the heat to a medium-low and simmer for 15 minutes. Drain the noodles in a colander set in the sink. Run cold water over them while you rub and swish them with your hand to rinse them. (This process gives the *udon* the desirable firm, chewy texture as well as removing excess starch, making the noodles slippery rather than sticky.) If using fresh *udon*, blanch by pouring just-boiled water over them in a bowl and leaving them for 5 minutes. Drain and set to one side.

Now make the sauce. Put the mirin in a saucepan and bring to the boil. Add the soy sauce, dashi and sugar, and mix well. Bring back to the boil, then remove from the heat and set aside to cool to room temperature (or, if you prefer it chilled, refrigerate).

Divide the noodles between 2 bowls. Scatter the bonito flakes and your chosen toppings on the noodles, then pour the sauce over the top. Serve with chopsticks and Chinese spoons.

Japanese-style Scallops with Soy Butter, Black Sesame and Somen Noodles (Japan)

As a typical South-east Asian, I don't eat an awful lot of dairy, but as I get older I've started to worry about the lack of calcium in my diet. I did some research and found out that sesame seeds contain a surprising amount of calcium. So here is a recipe for Japanese-style scallops using said seeds and even a bit of butter – delicious, and you can also feel like you're doing your bones some good. Osteoporosis be damned!

Serves 2 | Takes 20 minutes to make, 5 minutes to cook

large handful of sesame seeds (black, if possible)
200g dried thin Japanese wheat noodles (sōmen)
2 tbsp toasted sesame oil
1 tsp salt
large knob of unsalted butter, (about a heaped tbsp)
6 fresh fat scallops with coral
1 tbsp Japanese soy sauce (shoyu)
shichimi pepper (shichimi togarashi), to serve (optional)

Toast the sesame seeds in a dry frying pan over a medium-high heat for 5 minutes until fragrant, tossing occasionally so they don't stick or burn. Tip the seeds into a saucer and set to one side. (Don't wash the pan yet.)

Cook the noodles according to the packet instructions; drain, then dress with the sesame oil and salt. Set to one side.

Heat the butter in the frying pan over a high heat until sizzling. Add the scallops and sear for 2 minutes on each side. Sprinkle with the soy sauce, then toss the scallops in what is now a soy butter sauce.

Divide the dressed noodles between 2 shallow serving bowls. Top each with 3 scallops and sprinkle with the toasted sesame seeds and some shichimi pepper, if using. Serve with a green side salad.

Cook's Tips

Scallops often stick and leave a 'skin' in the frying pan. You can prevent this by making sure the scallops are not wet when they go into the pan. Dry by dabbing them with kitchen paper beforehand.

This dish is also really good with a Japanese sesame salt called *gomashio* sprinkled on the scallops, though slightly less pretty. Leave out the *shoyu*. Pound the toasted sesame seeds in a pestle and mortar to a fine powder, then mix with 1 teaspoon salt.

Spicy Chicken and Glass Noodle Salad

Yum Woon Sen (Thailand)

In this salad, popular throughout Thailand and also overseas, the noodles absorb the spicy sour dressing beautifully, and a different combination of flavours and textures greets you with every mouthful. This is traditionally served with a huge whack of chilli and a pint of beer. I also like to have it with steamed rice.

Serves 4 | Takes 1 hour to make, 10 minutes to cook

200g dried mung-bean thread noodles
8 dried shrimps
small handful of dried wood-ear mushrooms
1 tbsp groundnut oil
1 stalk lemongrass, trimmed of woody bits and finely sliced
1 leafy stalk of Chinese celery, stem thinly sliced and leaves shredded
100g minced chicken
12 large raw prawns, peeled, deveined and butterflied
1 red onion or 3 shallots, shaved thinly, soaked in cold water for 30 minutes and then drained
6 cherry or baby plum tomatoes, halved
2 fresh, red bird's eye chillies, finely sliced
2 tbsp salted peanuts, crushed

For the dressing
4 cloves garlic, peeled
1 stalk lemongrass, trimmed of woody bits
2 fresh coriander roots
4 tbsp fish sauce
1 tbsp light soy sauce
1 tbsp palm sugar or golden caster sugar
2 tbsp hot water
juice of 1 lime

To serve
1 small head of cos lettuce or 2 Baby Gem lettuces, leaves separated
sprigs of fresh coriander and mint
prawn crackers

Put the noodles, dried shrimps and mushrooms in 3 separate heatproof bowls and generously cover with just-boiled water. Leave them all to soak for 15 minutes. Drain the noodles and rinse with plenty of cold water, then set to one side. Drain the mushrooms, then slice and set aside. Drain the shrimps and set aside.

Combine all the dressing ingredients in a blender or food processor and blitz until the sugar has dissolved and the lemongrass and garlic are very finely chopped. Leave to mellow.

Heat the oil in a wok or frying pan on a medium-high heat. Add the sliced lemongrass and celery and stir-fry for 1–2 minutes until fragrant. Add the chicken and stir-fry for 3–4 minutes until it changes colour, breaking the meat up into small pieces as you go.

Then add the prawns and stir-fry for a further 2–3 minutes until they turn pink. Remove from the heat.

Put the noodles in a large salad or mixing bowl. Add the chicken and prawn mixture, mushrooms, shrimps, celery leaves, shaved onion, tomatoes, chillies and peanuts and toss together. Pour over the dressing and toss everything thoroughly to combine.

Divide the lettuce leaves among 4 pasta plates and add a portion of salad, then garnish with the coriander and mint and serve with prawn crackers. Or pile the salad on a large dish or platter, garnish with the herb sprigs and serve with the lettuce and prawn crackers on the side. In the latter case, give everyone a plate with a spoon and fork. Encourage them to scoop up the salad and wrap it up in the lettuce leaves.

Cook's Tip
This dish works equally well with minced pork (which is more traditional), turkey or even Quorn – I've used the latter for my pescatarian mother-in-law and she loves it.

Cold Sesame Noodles –

Liang Mian (China/Taiwan)

Here's more proof that salads needn't be boring. *Liang mian* (literally 'cold noodles') is a Sichuan dish of noodles dressed with sesame, peanuts, black vinegar and chilli. Other than these core ingredients, feel free to experiment because every street-vendor, restaurant and Sichuan cook will have his or her own recipe.

Serves 2 | Takes 20 minutes to make, 5 minutes to cook

200g fresh standard thick wheat noodles (*lo mein*) or 125g dried
3 cloves garlic, finely chopped
2 spring onions, thinly sliced (green and white parts kept separate)

For the dressing
1 tbsp Chinese sesame paste or tahini
$1/2$ tbsp chunky peanut butter
1 tbsp toasted sesame oil
1 tsp Chiu Chow chilli oil
2 tbsp chicken or vegetable stock
1 tbsp light soy sauce
$1/2$ tbsp dark soy sauce
2 tbsp Chinese black vinegar
$1/2$ tsp caster sugar

To garnish
$1/2$ Asian or Lebanese cucumber or $1/4$ regular cucumber, peeled, deseeded and julienned
handful of fresh coriander leaves, chopped
1 tsp toasted sesame seeds

Cook the noodles according to the packet instructions. Drain and rinse with cold water to stop the cooking process. Set to one side.

Whisk together the sesame paste, peanut butter, sesame oil and chilli oil in a large bowl or jug. Whisk the stock, soy sauces, vinegar and sugar in another bowl until the sugar dissolves. Whisking constantly, pour the contents of the second bowl slowly into the first bowl to combine the oily and non-oily ingredients.

Put the noodles, garlic and white parts of the spring onions in a salad bowl and add the sesame-peanut dressing. Mix thoroughly, then divide into 2 pasta bowls. Garnish each bowl with the green parts of the spring onions, the cucumber, coriander and the toasted sesame seeds. Serve immediately as a course on its own with chopsticks, or as an accompaniment.

Spiced Mung-bean Jelly Noodle Salad

Liang Fen (China)

This Chinese dish of mung-bean jelly noodles dressed with a sweet, sour and salty sauce is related to a Korean dish called *Nokdumuk*. There's also a similar dish in Burma made from rice flour, called *San Tohpu* (or 'rice tofu'), and another made from chickpea or gram flour, called *Tohpu Thohk* (or 'tofu salad') – Burmese tofu isn't made from soybeans like everyone else's. The jelly noodles here are super-easy and fun to make. Made from the same flour used for glass noodles, they're soft, light and translucent.

Serves 4 | Takes 3 hours to make, 5 minutes to cook

For the jelly noodles
70g mung-bean starch

For the dressing
2 tbsp groundnut oil
1 tsp Sichuan peppercorns
1cm piece of fresh ginger root, peeled
2 cloves garlic, finely chopped
$\frac{1}{2}$ tsp fermented black beans, finely chopped
2 tbsp light soy sauce
2 tbsp Chinese black vinegar
1 tsp caster sugar
1 tsp toasted sesame oil
1 tsp Chiu Chow chilli oil

To garnish
2 spring onions (white and green parts), julienned
handful of fresh coriander leaves, chopped
1 tbsp salted peanuts, crushed

First make the jelly noodles. Whisk the mung-bean starch with 250ml water in a jug or bowl until smooth. Bring 500ml water to the boil in a saucepan over a medium heat. With one hand, pour the mung-bean starch solution into the saucepan in a steady stream while whisking the contents of the pan with the other. At first, you'll find it easy to whisk the contents, but as the flour solution merges into the water, it will thicken and you'll meet with increasing resistance. Keep whisking steadily for a couple of minutes until the whole mix is thick and translucent. Remove from the heat.

Pour the resulting goo (I'm sorry, there is no other word for it) evenly into a greased 20 x 30cm baking tin. Smooth the surface, then leave to cool at room temperature for 30–45 minutes. Once cool, cover with clingfilm and chill for 2 hours until firm.

Meanwhile, make the Sichuan peppercorn oil. Heat the groundnut oil in a frying pan on a high heat and fry Sichuan peppercorns for 1–2 minutes until fragrant. Scoop out the peppercorns and discard. Leave the oil to cool, then pour into a jug.

Pound the ginger in a pestle and mortar with 2 tablespoons water to a pulp (or you can grate the ginger, then add 2 tablespoons hot water and mix). Squeeze the ginger in your hand over the jug containing the peppercorn oil, so the ginger juice runs in; discard the pulp. Add the rest of the dressing ingredients and whisk thoroughly together.

Remove the firm jelly from the fridge and slice into noodles of whatever size and shape you desire. I like to slice them into fat shards slightly larger than oven chips.

Spread the jelly noodles on a platter and drizzle the dressing over them. Garnish with the spring onions, coriander and peanuts. Give everyone a small bowl and chopsticks and tell them to help themselves.

Iced Buckwheat Noodles

Mul Naengmyeon (Korea)

Naengmyeon (also naengmyun or raengmyeon), meaning 'cold noodles', is a Korean dish of chilled buckwheat noodles served in a metal bowl with various toppings. There are two varieties: Mul Naengmyeon, which is served in a cold broth, and Bibim Naengmyeon, which is served with a spicy Korean pepper paste (gochujang) dressing. This recipe is for the former.

Serves 2 | Takes 20 minutes to make, 5 minutes to cook

200g Korean buckwheat noodles (naengmyeon)
1 Asian or Lebanese cucumber or 1/2 regular cucumber, peeled, deseeded and cut into matchsticks
1 Asian pear (nashi), peeled, cored and cut into matchsticks
1 1/2 tbsp caster sugar
1 tsp salt
500ml cold chicken stock
500ml cold beef stock
4 tbsp brown rice vinegar
6 ice cubes

To serve
2 soft-boiled eggs, cooled and peeled
sesame seeds
Korean mustard (gyeoja garu)

Cook the noodles according to packet instructions. Drain, rinse with plenty of cold water and set to one side.

Put the cucumber and pear into 2 separate bowls. Add 1/4 tablespoon each salt and sugar to both bowls and toss to mix. Set aside.

Combine the stock, vinegar and the remaining sugar and salt in a bowl and whisk together thoroughly. Add the ice cubes and set to one side.

Divide the noodles between 2 pasta plates. Pour over the iced broth (the ice cubes should be semi-melted) and top with the pear and cucumber. Add an egg to each plate, scatter sesame seeds on top and serve with Korean mustard on the side.

Simple Wheat Noodle Salad

Khao Swè Thohk (Burma)

There are various versions of *Khao Swè Thohk*, which just means 'noodle salad' in Burmese. My mother calls this one pauper's salad, because it's what they all lived off as students at Mandalay Medical School. In fact, the recipe she first related to me contained only 'noodles and a bit of oil'. But then, like the folkloric Nail Soup, she remembered more and more ingredients as time went on.

Serves 2 | Takes 10 minutes to make, 5 minutes to cook

150g dried standard thick wheat noodles (*lo mein*)
2 cloves garlic, peeled
4 tbsp Tamarind Juice (Secret Weapons, page 13)
$^1/_2$ tsp caster sugar
$^1/_2$ tsp chilli flakes
1 tbsp fish sauce
1 tbsp groundnut oil
$^1/_4$ tsp MSG or 1 tbsp Marigold bouillon powder
$^1/_4$ tsp salt

Cook the noodles according to the packet instructions; drain and set to one side in a large bowl.

Purée the garlic using a pestle and mortar or garlic press. Place in a jug or bowl and add the rest of the ingredients plus 50ml boiling water. Whisk until the sugar dissolves.

Pour the tamarind dressing over the noodles, mix thoroughly and serve immediately.

Mandalay Hand Mixed Noodles

Nan-gyi Thohk (Burma)

I remember watching *The Burma Road* at the age of nine, when I spied the presenter Miles Kington eating Mandalay *Mohntee* noodles – a delectable 'salad' of fat, blowsy rice noodles, chicken curry, chillies, leafy coriander and sharp raw onions. In raptures, I jumped up and shrieked to my mother, 'I KNOW that stall! I've BEEN to that stall! It's right next to grandma and grandpa's house! I'd kill to be there right now.' Mandalay *Mohntee* is more or less the same dish as *Nan-gyi Thohk* (literally 'big wire salad'), the only difference being that Mandalay *Mohntee* uses thick, round rice noodles and *Nan-gyi Thohk* uses flat, wide wheat noodles. Known as *nan-byar-gyi khao swè* ('flat big wire noodles'), these are similar to tagliatelle, which is what I've suggested you use. The dish is mixed by hand, and also traditionally eaten by hand, but you'd be forgiven for using a spoon and fork (but never chopsticks). Like many Burmese dishes, it's always served with a bowl of clear broth on the side.

Serves 4 | Takes 30 minutes to make, 3 hours 30 minutes to cook

400g dried tagliatelle

For the chicken broth and sauce
500g skinless chicken thighs (on the bone)
$1/4$ bunch of fresh coriander, stems very finely chopped to a paste and leaves chopped
2 cloves garlic, peeled
$1/2$ tsp MSG or 2 tbsp Marigold bouillon powder
1 tsp caster sugar
9 tbsp groundnut oil
3 medium onions, chopped
2 tbsp sweet paprika
2 tbsp ground turmeric
1 tsp hot chilli powder
freshly ground black pepper

For the garnishes
4 tbsp gram/chickpea flour
2 tbsp ground turmeric
200g ready-made fishcake, sliced
4 tbsp fish sauce
2 banana shallots or 1 small red onion, very thinly sliced, soaked in cold water for 30 minutes and drained
6 white cabbage leaves, shredded
4 soft-boiled eggs, cooled, peeled and halved
Fried Peanuts (Secret Weapons, page 11)
Fried Shallots (Secret Weapons, 11)

To serve
Chilli Oil (Secret Weapons, page 11)
lime wedges

Cook the tagliatelle according to the packet instructions until al dente. Drain in a colander and rinse thoroughly with cold water, then set to one side in the colander so that any residual water can continue to drain.

Now make the broth. Put the chicken, the coriander stems, garlic, half of the MSG (or bouillon powder) and the sugar in a medium saucepan with 1 litre water. Bring to the boil, then reduce the heat to medium-low and simmer for 1 hour, skimming any scum from the surface. Lift out the chicken, take the meat off the bone in large strips and set to one side (discard the bones). Keep the chicken broth warm.

Heat 3 tablespoons oil in another medium saucepan on a high heat. Add the onions and stir-fry for 3 minutes until fragrant. Reduce the heat to medium-low and add the remaining MSG (or bouillon powder), 100ml water, the paprika, turmeric and chilli powder. Mix thoroughly, then cook gently, stirring occasionally, for 1–2 hours until the onions have broken down completely. Now add a ladleful of the chicken broth and stir before popping the chicken meat into the sauce. Set the chicken sauce to one side but keep warm.

Toast the gram flour in a dry frying pan on a medium heat for 3–4 minutes until fragrant. (You must keep moving the pan so the flour shifts around, to avoid it catching and burning.) Tip into a bowl and set to one side.

Put the turmeric in a heatproof bowl. Heat 4 tablespoons oil in the frying pan on a high heat for a couple of minutes until sizzling, then pour on to the turmeric. Allow to settle before whisking to make turmeric oil. Set to one side.

Heat the remaining 2 tablespoons oil in the frying pan on medium heat. Add the fishcake and fry for 5 minutes until cooked. Set to one side.

Reheat the tagliatelle by placing the colander in your sink and pouring a kettleful of boiling water over them. Divide the tagliatelle among 4 pasta dishes. To each dish, add 1 tablespoon toasted gram flour, 3 tablespoons chicken sauce, 1 tablespoon turmeric oil and 1 tablespoon fish sauce. Now add some fishcake, sliced shallots, shredded cabbage and a soft-boiled egg. Lastly, sprinkle each dish with fried peanuts, fried shallots and chopped coriander leaves, and squeeze a wedge of lime over.

Bring the broth back to a simmer, then pour into 4 small soup bowls. Add some chopped coriander leaves and freshly ground black pepper to each bowl.

Serve the noodles immediately with forks and spoons (but do encourage your diners to get stuck in and use their hands to mix and eat the noodles!). Also serve the chilli oil and extra lime wedges for people to help themselves and the bowls of chicken broth with Chinese spoons on the side. This dish can also be eaten warm or at room temperature.

Burmese Rainbow Salad

Let Thohk Sohn (Burma)

This triple-carb beauty is called *Let Thohk Sohn* (or *Let Thoke Sone*), which literally means 'hand-tossed everything', but I've also seen it called 'rainbow salad', which, to be fair, seems more pleasant. It is perfect picnic fare as well as a pretty awesome desk lunch. Eaten cold or at room temperature, it's technically a salad (the Burmese for salad is *a-thohk*, ie 'tossed'), but its flavours and textures make it as far from a droopy bunch of green leaves as you can possibly imagine.

Serves 4–6 | Takes 30 minutes to make, 30 minutes to cook

200g dried mung-bean thread noodles
1 tbsp tomato purée
200g basmati rice
100ml Tamarind Juice (Secret Weapons, page 13)
2 medium floury potatoes, peeled
4 tbsp gram/chickpea flour
1 Shan fermented soybean cake (*tua nao*) (see Cook's Tip)
handful of dried shrimps
2 large carrots, julienned
2 white cabbage leaves, julienned
½ green papaya, peeled and julienned (optional)
Fried Peanuts (Secret Weapons, page 11)
groundnut oil
fish sauce

To garnish
handful of fresh coriander leaves, chopped
Fried Shallots (Secret Weapons, page 11)
Chilli Oil (Secret Weapons, page 11)

Put the noodles in a heatproof bowl, generously cover with just-boiled water and leave to soak for 15 minutes. Drain and rinse with plenty of cold water. Set to one side.

Cook the rice in a rice cooker or using the absorption method (see Cook's Tips), but add the tomato purée to the cooking water first – this tints the rice red and adds a hint of tomato flavour. Leave to cool and set to one side.

While the rice is cooking, cook the potatoes in a pan of boiling salted water until just tender. Drain and slice into fat discs, then set to one side.

Toast the gram flour by tossing in a dry frying pan on a medium-high heat for about 5 minutes until it smells fragrant. Tip into a bowl and set to one side.

If using the fermented soybean cake, toast it by tossing in the same dry frying pan on a medium-high heat for about 5 minutes until it smells fragrant. Tip into a mortar and grind into a powder with the pestle. Set to one side.

Grind the dried shrimps into a powdery fluff using a blender or food processor (or a pestle and mortar, though this will require some effort).

All the ingredients should be at room temperature at this point. Now the fun bit: get out a big salad bowl or mixing bowl and throw in all the prepared ingredients plus the carrots, cabbage, papaya and peanuts. Add a glug each of groundnut oil, tamarind juice and fish sauce (just enough for moisture) and mix lightly together using your hands. Alternatively, add a little bit of everything to each person's bowl, plus 1 tablespoon oil and 1 tablespoon fish sauce, and mix. Serve immediately, sprinkled with the garnishes, or keep, covered, for a few hours in the fridge or in a cool bag and scatter over the garnishes just before serving.

Cook's Tips

You can serve this in 2 ways – either ready-mixed or with all the ingredients in small dishes for diners to help themselves. It's much more fun to DIY though. The Burmese way with a lot of dishes is to adjust the flavourings according to taste – a bit more salt here, or a bit more sourness there – and you can get stuck right in yourself (remember it's called 'hand-tossed everything').

If you cannot get fermented soybean cake, you can substitute 1 tablespoon Chinese sesame paste or 1 tablespoon tahini mixed with 1 tablespoon peanut butter.

To cook basmati rice using the absorption method (aka the covered pan method), put 2 measures of water to 1 measure of rice into a medium saucepan (and, in this recipe, the tomato purée too). Bring to the boil. Stir the rice, then cover, reduce the heat to low and simmer for 10–12 minutes – the rice will absorb the water completely during this time. Do not be tempted to lift the lid or stir until the end, otherwise the steam that is cooking the rice will escape.

Once it is ready, remove the pan from the heat and leave to stand, still covered, for 5 minutes. The cooked rice will have craters in its surface – this is normal. Fluff with a fork and serve immediately, or leave to cool. The cooked rice can be kept, covered, in the fridge for 24 hours.

Sake-steamed Clams with Zero Noodles
(fusion)

If you've ever tried moules marinières, you'll know that seafood and white wine go together beautifully. Sake-steamed clams (*Asari No Sakamushi*) are, I suppose, the Japanese equivalent. This is far from an authentic version of this dish, however – the Japanese don't really use coriander or butter for a start – but the spirit is there. The flavours come together to make a dish that is fresh, light and almost summery. To add to the summery feel, *shirataki* noodles, made from the root of the devil's tongue yam or *konnyaku*, are virtually calorie-free, which is why they are also known as zero noodles or miracle noodles.

Serves 2 | Takes 15 minutes to make, 10 minutes to cook

1cm piece of fresh root ginger, peeled
2 cloves garlic, peeled
1 fresh, red bird's eye chilli
2 sprigs of fresh coriander
200g chilled shirataki or zero noodles, packed in water
1kg fresh clams in shell (palourdes are best)
100ml sake
2 tbsp mirin
15g butter (about 1 tbsp butter)
$\frac{1}{2}$ tsp caster sugar

Shred the ginger, garlic, chilli and coriander and put to one side. Scrub the clams under a running cold tap and discard any that don't shut when tapped sharply on the worktop. Set to one side.

Prepare the noodles according to the packet instructions, then drain and set to one side.

Put the clams in a wok or large saucepan and pour over the sake and 100ml water. Add the mirin, butter, sugar and shredded ginger and garlic. Cover with a lid and bring to the boil over a high heat, then reduce the heat and simmer for a few minutes until the clams have opened (discard any unopened clams).

Divide the noodles between 2 shallow serving bowls. Ladle the clams on to each portion, then drizzle the clam cooking juices over the top. Sprinkle with coriander and chilli, and serve immediately.

Prawn, Mizuna and Yuzu Salad

(fusion)

This salad is another one of those dishes that make you feel like you're doing yourself some good at the same time as being delicious. Try to track down the yuzu juice if you can – it will make this noodle salad sing.

Serves 2 | Takes 15 minutes to make, 5 minutes to cook

200g chilled shirataki or zero noodles, packed in water
12 large cooked prawns, peeled
handful of fresh mizuna leaves
1 fresh red finger chilli, deseeded and thinly sliced
1 spring onion, thinly sliced (green and white parts kept separate)

For the dressing
1 tbsp Japanese soy sauce (*shoyu*)
1 tbsp Dashi (page 9)
1 tsp mirin
1 tsp rice vinegar
1 tsp yuzu juice (see Cook's Tip)

Prepare the noodles according to the packet instructions, then drain, rinse with plenty of cold water and set to one side.

Whisk all the dressing ingredients together in a small jug or bowl.

Put the noodles, prawns, mizuna leaves, chilli and spring onion white parts in a mixing bowl and pour the dressing on top. Toss thoroughly together, then dish up into 2 pasta bowls. Scatter the spring onion greens on top and serve immediately, with forks.

Cook's Tip
To replace the yuzu juice, use $\frac{1}{2}$ teaspoon lime juice mixed with $\frac{1}{2}$ teaspoon orange juice. However, Waitrose now sell bottles of yuzu juice.

SNACKS

Steamed Pork and Mushroom Noodle Rolls
Bánh Cuốn (Vietnam)

Bánh Cuốn (literally 'rolled cake') is a breakfast dish from northern Vietnam. It is made from fermented rice batter, which is steamed on a cloth over a pot of boiling water to make extremely thin and delicate noodle sheets. These are then filled with pork, mushrooms and shallots and rolled up. The method here isn't as authentic but it's easier and you get to eat the noodle rolls much, much quicker, which is a plus in my book.

Makes 25–30 | Takes 1 hour 15 minutes to make, 30 minutes to cook

For the batter
200g rice flour
200g tapioca flour
$\frac{1}{2}$ tsp salt

For the filling
small handful of dried wood-ear mushrooms
groundnut oil
4 shallots, finely chopped
300g minced pork
1 tbsp fish sauce
1 tsp caster sugar
1 tsp freshly ground black pepper

To serve
Fried Shallots (Secret Weapons, page 11)
Vietnamese ham (*cha lua*), sliced
1 Asian or Lebanese cucumber or $\frac{1}{2}$ regular cucumber, peeled, deseeded and julienned
100g beansprouts, topped and tailed
Vietnamese Dipping Sauce (Secret Weapons, page 13)
fresh leafy herbs like coriander and shiso

Combine the batter ingredients in a large bowl, add 1 litre of water and whisk thoroughly. Set to one side.

Put the wood-ear mushrooms in a heatproof bowl, generously cover with just-boiled water and leave to soak for 15 minutes until soft. Drain and finely chop the mushrooms, then set to one side.

Heat 2 tablespoons oil in a wok or large frying pan on a medium-high heat and fry the shallots for 4–5 minutes until fragrant and translucent. Add the minced pork, mushrooms, fish sauce and sugar, and stir-fry for a further 5–6 minutes, breaking down the pork into small pieces as you go. Pour away any excess liquid or fat. Sprinkle with the pepper and toss to mix thoroughly, then set to one side.

Lightly brush some oil on to a large baking sheet (you'll be placing your noodle rolls on this).

Now heat a 28cm non-stick frying pan on a medium-high heat. Brush a light layer of oil on to the pan, then pour in a small ladleful of batter. Immediately tilt and swirl the pan in a circular motion so the batter spreads out to make a thin crêpe. Cover the pan with a lid and cook for 30–40 seconds, then flip the uncovered pan on to your oiled baking sheet so the crêpe falls out on to the sheet. (Don't worry if you mess up the first one – you'll soon get the hang of it.)

Add 1 tablespoon of the pork and mushroom filling to the crêpe and spread evenly. Fold in the left and right sides, then roll up gently into a flattish rectangular roll. Place on a serving dish. The noodle rolls should feel like silk to the touch and be translucent enough so that you can make out the filling inside.

Repeat until you've used up all the batter and filling to make 25–30 rolls – you will have to re-grease the frying pan and baking sheet every 3–4 crêpes. While you are filling and rolling one crêpe, ideally you should be making the next one.

When all the rolls have been made, chop each one into 3–4 pieces. Scatter the fried shallots all over them. Arrange the ham, cucumber and beansprouts on another dish and serve with the dipping sauce and herbs on the side.

Summer Rolls

Gỏi Cuốn (Vietnam)

Summer rolls are the quintessential Vietnamese snack. Fresh and light, stuffed with herbs and lettuce and other stuff, they are so deliciously good for you that this dish is practically a salad, but without the hair shirt. Classic fillings are thin rice noodles, lettuce, pork and prawns. The rolls sound tricky to make, but are actually very easy, as long as you have everything ready in advance.

Serves 4 | Takes 40 minutes to make

200g dried rice vermicelli noodles

12 large, round rice paper wrappers (20–22cm diameter)

250g cooked peeled king prawns (about 36)

1 velvet-leaved round lettuce (butterhead), leaves separated

250g cold shop-bought crispy roast pork (*siu yuk*) or roast duck (see Cook's Tip), diced

handful each of fresh mint and coriander leaves, plus – if you can get them – fresh Thai basil, cockscomb mint and shiso, roughly chopped

small bunch of fresh chives about 20cm long

Vietnamese Dipping Sauce (Secret Weapons, page 13), to serve

Put the rice noodles into a heatproof bowl, generously cover with just-boiled water and leave to soak for 20 minutes. Drain, then snip with scissors into chipolata-sized clumps and set to one side.

Fill a large, shallow container (big enough to hold a rice paper wrapper) with warm water.

Make the rolls one at a time. For each one, briefly dip a rice paper wrapper in the warm water, keeping the wrapper flat but making sure every part is moistened (see Cook's Tip for Vermicelli-stuffed Spring Rolls, page 142). Immediately lay the wrapper flat on the clean work surface.

The aim is to make a sausage-sized filling for the roll. Layer the ingredients on the wrapper as follows: first, place 3 prawns in a row across the middle. Fold a lettuce leaf to a shape to fit on the prawns and lay it in place. Add a clump of rice noodles on top of this and then a few chunks of roast pork or duck. Finish with a generous scattering of chopped herbs.

Place a chive (or, if they are slender, a few chives) along the top of the filling, so that one end sticks out over the edge of the wrapper. Fold the bottom edge of the wrapper over the filling and press down the edges, to make a rough semi-circle. Now fold over the side of the wrapper that doesn't have the chive sticking out of it, and press down. Finally, tightly roll up the whole summer roll like a fat cigar.

Repeat the procedure with the remaining rice paper wrappers and filling ingredients to make 12 rolls in total. When you've made all of them, you can serve immediately with the dipping sauce. If you're saving them for later, interleave them with foil or wrap them individually in clingfilm so they don't stick together, then pack gently into an airtight plastic container. Keep in the fridge so they don't dry out, and eat within a day.

Cook's Tips

I like to use diced roast pork belly (okay, so the claim to health food becomes wobbly here) or sometimes chunks of roast duck. You could use leftovers from any roast, if you like. Or you can even leave out the pork or duck to make the rolls meat-free, or substitute cold fried tofu.

As for herbs, you can play with the mix to some extent. The best combo uses chives and coriander but also slightly esoteric herbs like shiso, cockscomb mint and Thai basil, which give unexpected, citrussy, almost spicy notes. You can get away with just chives, coriander and mint however, and that will give the rolls just enough leafy pep.

Vermicelli-stuffed Spring Rolls

Chả Giò (Vietnam)

Chả giò is the Southern Vietnam name for the spring roll. In North Vietnamese communities, it's known as *nem rán*, which is why Asian traiteurs in Paris call their spring rolls 'nems'. Unlike most other spring rolls, its wrapper is made from rice paper rather than pastry. The fillings vary, but it's usually stuffed with a mix of noodles, mushrooms, minced meat and crunchy vegetables, to provide interesting contrasts.

Makes 20 | Takes 1 hour 15 minutes to make, 30 minutes to cook

20 round rice paper wrappers (16–18cm diameter)
groundnut oil, for deep-frying

For the filling

50g dried mung-bean thread noodles
small handful of dried wood-ear mushrooms
250g minced pork
100g cooked, peeled small prawns, finely chopped
100g cooked white crabmeat
1 carrot, julienned
2 shallots, finely chopped
2 cloves garlic, finely chopped
1 tbsp fish sauce
2 tsp caster sugar
1 tsp salt
¹/₂ tsp white pepper

To serve

Little Gem lettuce leaves
sprigs of fresh mint and coriander
Vietnamese Dipping Sauce (Secret Weapons, page 13)

Put the noodles in a heatproof bowl, generously cover with just-boiled water and leave to soak for 15 minutes. Drain and rinse with plenty of cold water. Snip with scissors into short sections and place in a large mixing bowl.

While the noodles are soaking, put the wood-ear mushrooms in a heatproof bowl, generously cover with just-boiled water and soak for 15 minutes until soft. Drain and finely chop the mushrooms, then add to the mixing bowl.

Add the rest of the filling ingredients to the bowl and mix thoroughly.

Fill a large, shallow container (big enough to hold a rice paper wrapper) with warm water.

Now it's time to assemble your spring rolls. Make them one at a time. For each, briefly dip a rice paper wrapper in the warm water, keeping the wrapper flat but making sure every part is moistened (see Cook's Tip). Immediately lay the wrapper flat on the clean work surface.

Add a heaped tablespoonful of the filling to the centre of the rice paper wrapper. Fold the bottom edge of the wrapper over the filling and press down the edges, to make a rough semi-circle. Tuck in the sides so they meet, then tightly roll up to form a cylinder about 7.5cm long.

Repeat the procedure with the remaining rice paper wrappers and filling to make 20 rolls in total.

Heat an 8cm depth of oil in a wok or large frying pan on medium-high heat. When you can feel waves of heat rising above it with the palm of your hand, gently place a few spring rolls in the wok – do not crowd them or let them touch one another, or they will split. Fry for 4–5 minutes, turning over halfway, until the wrapper puffs slightly and turns golden brown. Drain on parcel wrapping paper, leaving a gap between each roll (the spring rolls will stick to kitchen paper and turn soggy). Deep-fry the remaining rolls in the same way.

As soon as they all are ready, serve with the lettuce, herbs and sauce. You can just dip each spring roll in the sauce and eat, or roll up in a lettuce leaf with mint and coriander before dipping into the sauce.

Cook's Tip

Make sure you use warm and not hot water to moisten the rice paper wrappers – if the water is too hot, the wrappers will disintegrate into a gluey mess. You just need to dip the wrapper for a second or two (no need to drain) and then use it immediately.

Chinese Prawn 'Cannelloni'

Chee Cheong Fun (Hong Kong)

These noodle rolls from Hong Kong via China are like the big brother of *Bánh Cuốn* and my absolute favourite choice at a dim sum restaurant. Packed with prawns and drizzled with a sweet sauce, I'll happily fight anyone for the last piece. Don't be put off by the detailed instructions – these are fun and easy to make when you get the rhythm going. Incidentally, this is more or less how fresh *ho fun/kway teow* noodles are made. Just follow the recipe and then instead of keeping the pancakes whole, slice them into strips.

Makes 8–10 | Takes 40 minutes to make, 40 minutes to cook

25–30 large raw prawns, peeled and deveined

For the batter
150g rice flour
2 heaped tbsp cornflour
2 heaped tbsp tapioca flour
1 tbsp groundnut oil
1/2 tsp salt
2 spring onions (green parts only), finely chopped

For the sauce (*thim jeong*)
3 tbsp Indonesian sweet soy sauce (*kecap manis*)
1 tbsp light soy sauce
1 tbsp dark soy sauce
1 tbsp golden syrup
1 tbsp toasted sesame oil
2 tbsp boiling water

Mix the 3 flours together in a large bowl. Gradually add 500ml water in a slow stream while stirring. Now add the oil and salt and stir again. Set the batter aside to rest for 30 minutes.

Meanwhile, make the sauce. Combine all the ingredients in a jug and whisk to mix. Set to one side.

Lightly grease as many 20cm non-stick sandwich tins as you have. Set a rack or bamboo steamer in a wok full of water, or prepare a steamer that is large enough to accommodate a sandwich tin. Also prepare a bowl of iced water large enough to accommodate a sandwich tin.

Add the spring onion greens to the batter and mix well.

Bring the water in the wok to the boil on a high heat. Ladle enough batter into one of your greased cake tins to make a thin layer (about 3mm). Set the tin on the rack in the wok, put the lid on and steam for 3 minutes.

Remove the lid and scatter 3 prawns on top of the pancake that has formed. Cover again and steam for a further 2 minutes until the prawns turn pink. Lift out the tin and nestle it in the iced water bath to cool the pancake down quickly. Meanwhile, steam the next pancake.

When the edges of the pancake that's cooling down begin to pull away from the side of the tin, it's ready to roll. Tease up one of the edges, then roll up the pancake, encasing the prawns, and place it on a serving platter. The noodle rolls should be translucent enough so that you can just about make out the spring onion and prawns.

Repeat until you've made all the rolls. Then cut each one into 3–4 pieces and drizzle the sweet sauce over them. Serve with small plates and chopsticks, and tell everyone to tuck in.

Cook's Tip

If using a rack or bamboo steamer, make sure it is completely level in the wok, or you might pour too much batter into the sandwich tin and end up making a thick pancake that will break when you try to roll it up.

Persian Noodle Pie with Potato Crust

Tahdig (Iran)

Tahdig **(literally 'bottom of the pot') is a speciality of both Persian and Mesopotamian cuisine consisting of the crisp and golden rice crust taken from the bottom of the pot in which the rice is cooked. It's considered a treat so it's served up at meals and is offered to guests and loved ones first. Often thin slices of potato, carrot and even noodles are placed at the bottom of the pot instead of rice, so they will crisp up to form the** *tahdig***. A noodle crust can be difficult to perfect however, so here we have a noodle 'pie' with a potato** *tahdig***.**

Serves 4–6 | Takes 20 minutes to make, 1 hour 30 minutes to cook

300g dried bucatini
7 tbsp groundnut oil
1 medium onion, chopped
3 cloves garlic, chopped
1 tsp ground turmeric plus an extra pinch
300g minced beef
1 large ripe tomato, peeled and chopped
1 tbsp tomato purée
small handful of fresh flat-leaf parsley, chopped
1 large floury potato, peeled and sliced into rounds
salt and pepper to taste

Cook the bucatini noodles in a large pot of boiling salted water until they bend but still have a chalky middle (I suggest 2–3 minutes short of the cooking time recommended on the packet). Drain, rinse with cold water and set to one side.

Heat 2 tablespoons oil in a saucepan on a medium-high heat. Fry the onion for 5–6 minutes until translucent, then add the garlic and fry for a further 2–3 minutes. Stir in 1 teaspoon turmeric and fry for 1–2 minutes until fragrant. Now add the beef and brown for 6–7 minutes, breaking it up into small piece as you go.

Tip out any excess fat before adding the chopped tomato, tomato purée and 100ml water. Mix well. Turn the heat to high. When the mixture starts to sizzle and boil, reduce the heat to medium-low and simmer for 20 minutes until excess liquid has evaporated. Season with salt and pepper to taste, then stir the chopped parsley into the meat sauce.

Heat 3 tablespoons oil in a large, non-stick, heavy-bottomed saucepan on a high heat for a minute. Add a pinch of turmeric and swirl the spiced oil in the pan to coat the bottom evenly. Remove from the heat.

Lay the sliced potato rounds in the bottom of the pan so that it's completely covered. Now add a layer of noodles, and then a layer of the meat sauce. Keep alternating the layers until you've used everything up, making sure you end with a top layer of noodles.

Drizzle the remaining 2 tablespoons oil over the noodles, then place a soft tea towel over the top of the pan followed by the lid (make sure the towel doesn't hang down the sides). Set the pan back on a high heat for a minute (to help start off the potato crust), then reduce the heat to medium-low and leave to cook for 45 minutes.

Remove the lid and the tea towel. Place a large plate or platter upside-down over the saucepan. Holding them firmly together (wear oven gloves or use the tea towel), carefully turn the saucepan over to unmould the noodle pie on to the plate, with its potato crust intact. Cut the noodle pie into wedges and eat immediately.

Five Spice Ribbon Noodle Crisps

(fusion)

This is a fun alternative to popcorn and ready in minutes. Experiment with seasonings – garam masala, chilli, or even salt and icing sugar for the real cinema experience.

Serves 4–6 | Takes 5 minutes to make, 5 minutes to cook

200g dried broad, flat rice noodles (*ho fun*)
groundnut oil for deep-frying
1 tsp five spice powder
1 tsp salt
1 tsp freshly ground black pepper

Break the dried noodles into 5cm pieces. Heat a 6cm depth of oil in a wok or deep frying pan on a high heat. When you can feel waves of heat coming off it with the palm of your hand, toss in one of the noodle pieces. If it puffs up immediately like a prawn cracker, the oil is ready.

Turn the heat down slightly, then scatter a small handful of noodles into the wok, making sure not to crowd them. Watch the noodles puff up and cook in seconds. As soon as they do so, remove them with a slotted spoon and drain on kitchen paper. Repeat the process until you have fried all the noodles.

When they're cool, put them in a large bowl. Sprinkle the five spice, salt and pepper over them and toss gently so they're evenly covered. Eat immediately or keep in an airtight container for up to a week.

Japanese Noodle Omelette
Omusoba (Japan)

This dish, like its more famous sibling *Omurice*, is a typical example of Japanese ingenuity. How do you make *yakisoba* noodles more entertaining? Why, wrap them in an omelette! (From this, you may deduce that *Omurice* is fried rice wrapped in an omelette.) You can even find *omusoba-pan* in restaurants in Japan – that's *yakisoba* noodles wrapped in an omelette and then in a bread roll. Sounds crazy, but it's awesome.

Serves 2 | Takes 20 minutes to make, 30 minutes to cook

75g dried standard thick wheat noodles (*lo mein*) or 150g fresh ramen noodles (*chūkamen*)
3 tbsp groundnut oil
1/2 medium onion, sliced
100g pork belly, thinly sliced, or 1 boneless, skinless chicken thigh, cut into small strips
2 Savoy cabbage leaves, sliced
50g beansprouts, topped and tailed
2 tbsp sake or water
4 eggs, beaten and seasoned with a pinch of salt and pepper
salt and pepper to taste

For the *yakisoba* sauce
6 tbsp Japanese soy sauce (*shoyu*)
6 tbsp Worcestershire sauce or HP sauce
3 tbsp tomato ketchup
1 tsp freshly ground black pepper

To garnish
Japanese mayonnaise
powdered nori seaweed (*aonori*)

If using dried noodles, cook according to the packet instructions; drain and rinse with cold water. If using fresh ramen noodles, just loosen them. Set the noodles aside.

Combine the *yakisoba* sauce ingredients in a small bowl or jug and whisk together.

Heat 1 tablespoon oil in a wok or large frying pan on medium heat. Add the onion and stir-fry for 1–2 minutes. Add the pork or chicken and stir-fry for 3–4 minutes until it changes colour and loses its raw look. Add a pinch each of salt and pepper and toss.

Now add the cabbage to the wok and stir-fry for another 3–4 minutes. Add the beansprouts and stir-fry for a minute before adding the noodles. Pour the sake over everything and toss for 1–2 minutes, then add half the *yakisoba* sauce and mix well to ensure it is distributed evenly. Set the wok to one side, but keep warm.

Heat 1 tablespoon oil in a large frying pan on a medium-high heat. Pour in half the beaten eggs and leave for 1–2 minutes so the eggs set slightly into an omelette, then spoon half the noodle mix on top. Flip one side of the omelette over to fold it in half and encase the noodles. Cook for another minute before dishing up on to a warm plate. Keep warm while you make the second omelette.

Drizzle mayonnaise and the rest of the *yakisoba* sauce over the noodle-filled omelettes and sprinkle with powdered seaweed. Serve immediately, with spoons and forks.

Soba Noodles with Dipping Sauce
Zaru Soba (Japan)

These chilled noodles make for a really simple but refreshing dish – perfect for when you just want a light meal. There is a bit of ritual in how you should eat them: you use your chopsticks to pick up a mouthful of noodles, and then you dip them into the sauce and then in the garnishes. The cold dipping sauce, known as *mentsuyu*, is also used as a soup stock when hot. Ideally you should serve your noodles in a bamboo sieve or basket (this is the *zaru* in the recipe name) but it's really not necessary.

Serves 4 | Takes 15 minutes to make, 20 minutes to cook

180g dried Japanese buckwheat noodles (*soba*)
50ml mirin
350ml Dashi (page 9)
50ml dark soy sauce
1 tbsp caster sugar
handful of dried nori seaweed strips
wasabi paste
1cm piece of fresh root ginger, peeled and grated
4 spring onions (green and white parts), finely sliced into rings

Bring a saucepan of water to the boil. Scatter the noodles into the water, then immediately turn the heat down to medium-low and simmer for 15 minutes. Drain in a colander and run cold water over the noodles, rubbing and swishing them with your hand to rinse them well. (This process gives the soba the desirable firm, chewy texture as well as removing excess starch, making the noodles slippery rather than sticky.) Leave the noodles to drip-dry in the colander.

Heat the mirin in a saucepan on a medium heat for 5 minutes. Add the dashi, soy sauce and sugar and bring to the boil. Remove from the heat and leave this dipping sauce to cool completely.

Arrange the noodles in neat bundles on 4 plates or *zaru* and garnish with the seaweed. Divide the dipping sauce among 4 small bowls (deep Chinese tea cups are ideal). Put the wasabi, ginger and spring onions on 4 saucers and serve them on the side.

Hiroshima Noodle Pancake

Hiroshima Okonomiyaki (Japan)

The name of this savoury pancake from Japan is derived from *okonomi*, meaning 'what you like' and *yaki* meaning 'grilled' or 'cooked'. This is because, at restaurants and street vendors alike – even here in the UK – you can choose from a range of toppings and fillings, and even make it yourself on a tabletop hotplate. The Hiroshima version is famous for its use of noodles as a filling. So beloved is *Okonomiyaki* there, they even have a food theme park called *Okonomi-mura* that is dedicated to the stuff.

Serves 2 | Takes 30 minutes to make, 30 minutes to cook

groundnut oil
200g fresh ramen noodles
   (*chūkamen*)

For the batter
60g self-raising flour, sifted
120g fresh Japanese taro
   (*nagaimo*), peeled and grated
60ml Dashi (page 9)
1/4 tsp caster sugar
1/4 tsp salt

For the filling
200g white cabbage, shredded
handful of beansprouts,
   topped and tailed
6 rashers streaky bacon
2 eggs

For the toppings
ready-made *Okonomiyaki*
   sauce (see Cook's Tip)
Japanese mayonnaise

2 spring onions (green and
   white parts), thinly sliced
bonito flakes (*katsuobushi*)
Japanese red pickled ginger
   (*beni shoga*)
powdered nori seaweed
   (*aonori*)

Mix together the batter ingredients in a bowl and set to one side.

The ideal way to cook this dish is on a hotplate. Or you can use 2 large frying pans or smooth griddle pans, alternating the cooking of the stages between them. Preheat the hotplate to medium-low, then smear with a thin layer of oil (or heat 1 tablespoon oil in the first frying pan on a medium-low heat and swirl the oil so the bottom of the pan is evenly covered).

Using a ladle, pour a little less than half the batter on to the hotplate (or oiled pan) in a circular motion to form a pancake about 15–20cm in diameter. Scatter some bonito and seaweed over the pancake. Turn the heat up to medium and scatter half the cabbage and half the beansprouts over the pancake, then lay 3 rashers of bacon on top (side by side). Finally, drizzle 1 tablespoon batter over everything to 'glue' it all together. Leave the pancake to cook for 6–7 minutes to form a golden crust on the base.

Flip the pancake over quickly but gently, using 2 spatulas, and press it down hard, tucking in any rogue bits of vegetable (the bacon layer is now at the bottom). Cook for another 6–7 minutes to make sure the vegetables are tender and the bacon is cooked.

Meanwhile, on another section of the hotplate (or in the second frying pan on a medium heat), stir-fry half the ramen noodles with 1 teaspoon oil and a drizzle of *Okonomiyaki* sauce for 5 minutes until cooked.

Form the noodles into a disc the same size as the pancake. Lift the pancake with a spatula (the bacon should have formed a solid base) and place it on top of the noodles.

Heat 1 tablespoon oil on the hotplate (or in the first frying pan). Crack in an egg; break the yolk and spread it out so it covers the white. Now lift the pancake with a spatula (the noodles should have formed a crust on the base), place it on top of the egg and press down firmly. Leave to cook for 30 seconds, then flip again so the pancake is at the bottom and the fried egg on top.

Keep warm while you make the second pancake in the same way.

When both pancakes are ready, slide them on to plates. Pipe or drizzle the *Okonomiyaki* sauce and mayonnaise in a criss-cross pattern over the pancakes (you can use a toothpick or fork to create a cobweb pattern rather like on a cream slice).

Scatter the spring onions, bonito flakes and pickled ginger on top, sprinkle with the seaweed and serve immediately. In Japan, they use the cooking spatulas to chop the pancakes into small pieces and then they eat them with chopsticks, but I think you can be forgiven for using a knife and fork.

Cook's Tip
Look for ready-made *Okonomiyaki* sauce in Japanese supermarkets, or you can use Tonkatsu Sauce (Secret Weapons, page 13).

Cheat's Bombay Mix

Chevda (fusion)

My father used to be obsessed with Bombay mix – I'd often find him reading with a bowl of the stuff by his side. This Indian snack's proper name is *Chevda*, and it consists of a moveable feast of spicy dried ingredients flavoured with salt and spices. One thing it always seems to contain is *sev* – fried noodles made from lentils. You need a special gadget to extrude these bad boys though, so I thought of this easy short-cut. It's addictive, I tell thee.

Serves 2–4 | Takes 5 minutes to make, 40 minutes to cook, plus overnight soaking the day before

4 tbsp dried green lentils
4 tbsp dried chickpeas
50g dried thick, round rice noodles (Vietnamese *bún* or Guilin rice vermicelli)
groundnut oil for deep-frying
4 tbsp raw peanuts (skin on)
1 individual packet of ready-salted crisps

For the spice mix
$\frac{1}{2}$ tsp each ground cumin, coriander, turmeric, sumac, caster sugar, chilli powder and salt

Soak the lentils and chickpeas in separate bowls of water overnight. The next day, drain in a sieve and allow to drip-dry as thoroughly as possible.

Snap the dried noodles into 2cm pieces and set to one side.

Heat a 5cm depth of oil in a wok on a medium-high heat (or use a deep-fat fryer). When you can feel waves of heat rising above it with the palm of your hand, gently add the soaked lentils and step back – any residual water in the soaked lentils will make the oil spit and cause steam. The lentils will take 8–10 minutes to cook – you'll know they're ready when they rise up in the oil, and their skins begin to come away. Carefully remove the pan from the heat and scoop out the lentils with a slotted spoon on to kitchen paper. Leave to drain and cool – they will crisp up as they cool.

Reheat the oil and fry the chickpeas in the same way, again taking care when you add them. The chickpeas will take longer to cook – 10–15 minutes. Scoop out and drain on kitchen paper. They will crisp up as they cool.

Reheat the oil once more, then toss the noodles into the wok. They should puff up immediately like prawn crackers. As soon as they do, scoop them out with a slotted spoon and drain on kitchen paper.

Pour away most of the oil (reserve for use in other recipes), leaving about 1 tablespoon in the wok. Reheat the wok on a medium heat, then fry the peanuts, tossing them, for about 10 minutes until they smell fragrant and their skins have become darker red and shiny. Scoop out and drain on kitchen paper. When they cool down, they will be crunchy.

When the fried pulses, noodles and peanuts have all cooled down, combine in a large bowl. Smash up the crisps into small pieces and add to the bowl. Add all the spices and toss thoroughly to ensure even coverage. The mix can be stored in an airtight container for up to a month.

Ramen Burger

(Japan)

Made popular by Keizo Shimamoto, writer of the blog *Go Ramen!* and now ramen chef in Brooklyn, the ramen burger is a curious thing – sister to the Japanese chain MOS Burger's famous rice burger, it uses ramen noodles as the unlikely burger receptacle (the ramen is the burger bun). Like MOS Burger, its roots come from Japan, though its forerunner is more traditional in that all the usual elements are there, including *cha shu* pork, *naruto* fishcake, *menma* bamboo shoots and spring onions. My version takes the ramen burger back to Japan, using pork, Japanese mushrooms, spring onions, *tonkatsu* sauce and shichimi pepper. It's a bit of a faff, but I think it's worth the effort.

Serves 2 | Takes 45 minutes to make, 20 minutes to cook

2 individual packets of instant noodles eg Super Noodles, Nissin, Koka or Maggi (flavour of your choice)
1 tbsp toasted sesame oil
1 egg, beaten with 1 tbsp water
1 eringi mushroom, sliced
200g poached pork belly or shop-bought Chinese barbecue pork (*char siu*), sliced
2 spring onions (green and white parts), julienned
Tonkatsu Sauce (Secret Weapons, page 13)
shichimi pepper (*shichimi togarashi*)

Slightly over-cook the noodles in a pan of boiling water for 8–10 minutes; drain. Each packet comes with a sachet of seasoning – mix just one of these into the noodles along with the sesame oil. Leave to cool for 5 minutes before adding the egg and stirring through so that the noodles are coated. They will congeal, which is what you want.

Divide the noodles into 4 portions and pack into 4 ramekins, cooking rings, burger moulds or other round containers lined with greaseproof paper. Put a circle of greaseproof paper on top of each noodle patty, then set a smaller container on top of this to press the patties down. (I also weigh each down with a can of beans.) Chill for 30 minutes.

Heat 1 tablespoon oil in a large frying pan on a high heat until sizzling, then fry the mushroom slices for 2 minutes. Remove and set to one side.

Heat another tablespoon of oil in the pan on a high heat until sizzling, then turn down to a medium heat. Uncover the noodle patties and unmould into the pan. Fry for 3 minutes on each side. Apart from flipping them once, do not be tempted to move the noodle patties – you want to avoid collapse, and they need to form a brown crust.

Flip the patties on to 2 plates and snip off any rogue noodles if necessary. Top one of each pair of patties with some pork, the mushroom slices, some spring onions, some tonkatsu sauce and some shichimi pepper. Set the other noodle patty on top and eat immediately.

New Year's Eve Noodles

Toshikoshi Soba (Japan)

How better to end this collection of noodle-based goodness than with a recipe for New Year's Eve Noodles? Unlike in the West, the Japanese celebrate New Year's Eve quietly, to reflect on the year that's ending. Late in the evening, whilst waiting to greet the new year, the traditional meal is a small bowl of these hot *soba* noodles – *toshikoshi* roughly means 'end the old year and enter the new year'. There is no set recipe for the toppings, which can be as simple or elaborate as you wish. Make sure you don't cut your noodles though, as their length represents longevity and therefore a wish for a happy life.

Serves 2 | Takes 25 minutes to make, 25 minutes to cook

750ml Dashi (page 9)
50ml mirin
1 tsp granulated sugar
100ml Japanese soy sauce (*shoyu*)
90g dried Japanese buckwheat noodles (*soba*)
150g Japanese fishcake (*kamaboko* or *naruto*), thinly sliced
handful of Tempura Crumbs (*tenkasu*), (Secret Weapons, page 13)
2 spring onions (green and white parts), sliced into thin rings
handful of dried nori seaweed strips
shichimi pepper (*shichimi togarashi*)

Combine the dashi and mirin in a saucepan. Bring to the boil, then turn the heat to medium-low and simmer gently for 3–4 minutes. Add the sugar and let it dissolve before adding the soy sauce. Set the pan of broth to one side.

Bring a saucepan of water to the boil. Scatter the noodles into the water, then immediately turn the heat down to medium-low and simmer for 15 minutes. Drain in a colander and run cold water over the noodles, rubbing and swishing them with your hand to rinse them well. (This process gives the *soba* the desirable firm, chewy texture as well as removing excess starch, making the noodles slippery rather than sticky.) Leave the noodles to drip-dry in the colander.

When ready to serve, divide the noodles between 2 noodle bowls. Add the fishcake slices to the saucepan of broth and simmer on a medium heat for 4–5 minutes. Ladle the broth over the noodles, arranging the fishcake artfully on top. Garnish each bowl with tempura crumbs, spring onions and seaweed strips, and sprinkle shichimi pepper on top. Serve immediately with chopsticks.

Glossary and Stockists

For more detailed information, see the notes in the introduction. Note that most ingredients can be found in oriental or Asian supermarkets and even larger branches of Western supermarkets. Others can be found in supermarkets that cater for the specific cuisine, such as Vietnamese or Japanese stores or online.

Anchovy Small fish commonly salted in brine and packed in oil; *ikan bilis* is the common name (originally Malaysian) for the tiny, dried version used in stocks and sambals.

Annatto Red spice used to add colour and a little heat in Vietnamese dishes.

Aonori Powdered nori seaweed used as a garnish.

Asam keping See dried mangosteen peel

Asian pear (*nashi*) Round with crisp, slightly sweet flesh.

Asian cucumber Small, with knobbly skin, firm, dense flesh and few seeds; similar to Lebanese cucumber.

Asian shallot Small pink shallot, about the size of a clove of garlic.

Bagoong See Shrimp paste
Bai kaprao See Holy basil
Bai horapha See Thai basil

Bamboo shoot Can be found dried, pickled or in brine; *menma* are Japanese pickled bamboo shoots.

Banana blossom Bud of the banana plant; sold as whole fresh buds in Asian and Indian supermarkets, or fresh and sliced in packets in Vietnamese supermarkets.

Banana shallot (echalion) Long, bulb-like cross between an onion and a shallot.

Beancurd puffs (*tau pok*) Also known as tofu puffs, these are fried puffed tofu pieces.

Beancurd skin (tofu skin, yuba, beancurd sheet) Thin dried sheets of tofu sold in packets; they need to be rehydrated before use.

Beech mushroom *See* Shimeji mushroom

Beef balls Meatballs made of pounded beef mixed with flour; have a springy texture. Sold fresh or frozen, usually in packets of 12; normally boiled. Often contains beef tendon to add to the springy texture.

Beef tendon Tissue that connects muscle to bone; when lightly cooked, valued for its gelatinous, chewy nature in Asian beef dishes.

Belacan See Shrimp paste

Beni shoga See Japanese red pickled ginger

Bird's eye chilli Small, red or green fiery chilli from South-east Asia (red is preferred for the colour).

Black prawn paste (*hae ko, petis udang*) Thick, sweetened, black paste with a consistency like treacle; used as a condiment for Tamarind Fish Laksa and other dishes in Malaysia, Indonesia and Singapore. *See also* Shrimp paste

Bonito Type of fish that is dried and then shaved into wafer-thin flakes called *katsuobushi*; used as a garnish as well as the base for dashi.

Bottle gourd (calabash) Vine fruit that can be picked young, peeled and eaten in soups, stews or stir-fries, or picked when mature, hollowed out and dried, and used as a bottle (hence the name). When fresh, it has pale green, smooth skin and white flesh that turns translucent when cooked. Cucumber can be used as a substitute.

Candlenut Rich waxy nut, similar to macadamia nut.

Cassia bark Dried spice, similar to cinnamon but slightly sweeter and stronger; sold in sticks or ground in jars.

Cha lua Vietnamese ham, similar to Polish sausage in texture; sold in fat rolls for slicing.

Cha shu Japanese braised pork belly; it is an adaptation of Chinese *char sui* hence the name is a corruption. Common ingredient in ramen dishes.

Char sui See Chinese barbecue pork
Chikuwa See Japanese fishcake

Chilli bean sauce (*là doubanjiang*) *Salty, fiery paste made from fermented broad beans, soya beans, chillies, salt, rice and spices.*

Chilli oil Unlike Western-style chilli oil, which tends to be oil infused with dried chillies, Asian-style chilli oil comprises crushed dried red chillies that are deep-fried and then stored in the oil they were fried in. Common table condiment, available in jars in most supermarkets, or *see* recipe on page 11.

Chinese barbecue pork (*char siu*) Pork fillet with a sweet red glaze made from honey, five-spice powder, red fermented bean curd, dark soy sauce and hoisin sauce; found hanging in strips at Chinese restaurants.

Chinese black vinegar Dark, sweet and mild vinegar. Chinkiang is the best type.

Chinese broccoli (*kai-lan, gailan*) Green leafy vegetable with small florets, similar to regular broccoli or calabrese.

Chinese celery Similar to regular celery, but stronger in flavour and more yellow.

Chinese rice wine Dry cooking wine similar to dry sherry. Shaoxing is the best type.

Chinese sausage (*lap cheong*) Dried fatty, sweet and chewy sausage; sold in bundles; usually fried.

Chinese sesame paste Dark rich paste made from roasted sesame seeds.

Chiu Chow chilli oil Savoury chilli oil with extra bits/sediment such as sugar and salt; used as a condiment; sometimes called crispy chilli. Lao Gan Ma is the best brand.

Choy sum Green leafy vegetable, similar to spinach.

Coriander One of Asia's most versatile herbs since its leaves, seeds, stems and even roots are all used for cooking.

Curry roux Japanese instant curry cubes; sold in boxed blister packs. House and S&B are the best brands.

Daikon (mooli) Long, large white radish.

Dashi Japanese stock usually made from kombu seaweed and bonito flakes. Instant dashi granules are sold in tubs or in individual sachets in Japanese supermarkets.

Dried mangosteen peel The dried skin of a type of mangosteen called *asam keping* or *asam gelugur* in Malaysian; thought by some to be an essential ingredient in Tamarind Fish Laksa. Available in packets.

Dried onion or shallot flakes Used to make fried shallots (*see* Secret Weapons on page 11); found in packets or tubs.

Dried red kapok flower (*dok ngiao*) Flower from the *Bombax ceiba* tree, thought by some to be an essential ingredient in Dai Meat and Tomato Noodles; unavailable outside of South-east Asia.

Dried shrimps Tiny dried prawns sold in packets.

Dried Thai chilli (*prik haeng*) Dried whole red chillies sold in packets in oriental supermarkets. Similar in appearance to finger chillies; medium heat.

Eringi mushroom (king trumpet, French horn or king oyster mushroom) Fresh, meaty mushroom with a large stem.

Fermented black beans Dried soya beans that have been fermented with salt; sold in packets. Can substitute Chinese black bean sauce in jars found in Western supermarkets.

Finger chilli Long, thin red or green chilli.

Fish sauce Amber-coloured liquid made from fermented fish and salt; *nam pla* in Thai, *nước mắm* in Vietnamese, *patis* in Filipino, *ngan bya yay* in Burmese; used as a table condiment as well as cooking ingredient. Viet Hoa Three Crabs is by far the best brand.

Fish ball Made of pounded fish mixed with flour; has a springy texture. Sold fresh or frozen, usually in packets of 12; normally boiled.

Fishcake Asian-style fishcake is made of pounded fish mixed with flour; has a spongy texture. Usually comes in a 'brick' that is sliced to order; normally boiled or fried. *See also* Japanese fishcake

Flying fish roe (*tobiko*) Tiny, jewel-like orange fish eggs; sold fresh in Japanese supermarkets.

Fried shallots Asian shallots that have been fried until crisp and crunchy; used as a garnish. Sold in tubs, or *see* Secret Weapon recipe on page 11.

Galangal Root or rhizome similar to ginger but more aromatic; can be used fresh or dried.

Garam masala Mixture of ground spices, similar to curry powder, but individual spices are generally identifiable.

Garlic chive (Chinese chive) Green herb with long flat stalks; garlicky version of regular chives.

Glutinous rice flour Ground from glutinous rice, used as a thickener and in some noodles.

Gochujang See Korean pepper paste
Gomashio Japanese sesame and salt seasoning.

Gram flour (chickpea flour) Used as a thickener or flavouring agent.

Hbè bohk See Shan fermented soybean cake
Hoisin sauce Thick, sweet, salty dipping sauce made from fermented soya beans.
Holy basil (Thai holy basil, *bai kaprao, kraphao*) Hot, fresh purple herb essential for Drunken Noodles.
Húng quế See Thai basil

Ikan bilis See Anchovy
Ikura See Salmon roe
Indonesian sweet soy sauce (*kecap manis*) Thicker and sweeter than regular soy sauce.

Japanese egg (*tamago*) The following Japanese-style eggs appear in this book: *onsen tamago* (literally 'hot spring' egg), *nitamago* (ramen egg) and *kinshi tamago* (crepe-like omelette).
Japanese fermented soya beans (*natto*) Salty and savoury with an unusual sticky texture; sold frozen (thaw to use). Traditionally eaten at breakfast on rice rather than used an ingredient, but a good substitute for Shan fermented soybean cake.
Japanese fishcake *Chikuwa* are short, spongy fishcake tubes, sometimes with brown bands around the middle; *kamaboko* and *naruto* come as 'logs' of springy fishcake, which are sliced before using. Cross-section slices of *kamaboko* are generally half-moon-shaped, sometimes with a pink border; cross-section slices of *naruto* are flower-shaped with a pink swirl. All Japanese fishcake is sold fresh and frozen, and is generally simmered in stock before eating.
Japanese mayonnaise Sweeter and more savoury than Western mayonnaise (egg yolks are used instead of whole eggs). The only brand to use is Kewpie.
Japanese mustard (*karashi*) Yellow mustard sold as paste or in powdered form; similar to English mustard.
Japanese red pickled ginger (*beni shoga, kizami shoga*) Ginger that has been peeled, julienned and pickled in sugar, purple shiso and the leftover juices from Japanese salt-pickled apricots (*umeboshi*).
Japanese taro (*nagaimo*) Edible tuber or root with unusual sticky flesh; used fresh.
Japanese soy sauce (*shoyu*) Slightly sweet, halfway between light and dark soy sauce. Kikkoman is the best brand.

Kaffir lime Small fragrant lime whose leaves are used fresh or dried in cooking.
Kai-lan See Chinese broccoli
Kamaboko See Japanese fishcake
Kapi See Shrimp paste
Karashi See Japanese mustard
Katsuobushi See Bonito
Kecap manis See Indonesian sweet soy sauce
Kelp Seaweed used dried.
Khao swè The Burmese word for noodle.
Kikurage See wood-ear mushroom
Kimchi Korean fermented pickle. See my easy recipe on meemalee.com
Kinshi tamago See Japanese egg
Kizami shoga See Japanese red pickled ginger
Kombu Japanese dried seaweed used to make dashi. Normally sold in packets of sheets or strips, but sometimes sold tied in knots for simmering directly in soup.
Korean pepper paste (red pepper paste, hot pepper paste, *gochujang*) Fermented condiment misnamed as it is made from red chilli (rather than peppers), glutinous rice, fermented soya beans and salt.
Korean mustard (*gyeoja garu*) Yellow mustard sold as paste or in powdered form; hotter than English mustard.

Laksa leaf See Vietnamese coriander
Lap cheong See Chinese sausage
Lemongrass Aromatic grass sold fresh in thick stalks or as a paste (the latter pales in comparison, so try to buy fresh).
Lily flowers Dried lily buds, sold in packets.
Liquid aminos Liquid seasoning that makes dishes more savoury in the same way that sugar makes dishes sweeter or salt makes dishes saltier.
Lontong Compressed rice cubes
Luffa (Vietnamese gourd, *patola*) Vine fruit that can be picked young, peeled and eaten in soups, stews or stir-fries, or picked when mature, dried and used as a sponge (when it is known as a loofah). When fresh, it has pale green, ridged skin and white flesh that turns translucent when cooked. Cucumber can be used as a substitute.

Maggi seasoning Liquid seasoning that makes dishes more savoury in the same way that sugar makes dishes sweeter or salt makes dishes saltier.
Mắm ruốc See Shrimp paste
Mein, Mian The Chinese word for noodles.

Men-tsuyu (tsuyu) Japanese noodle dipping sauce used with chilled *udon* and *soba* dishes; can be bought in bottles.
Mirin Japanese sweet rice wine used in cooking.
Miso Japanese fermented soya bean paste used in cooking; the darker the miso, the stronger and sweeter it is. Both red (*aka miso*) and white (*shiro miso*) are available in the refrigerator section of Japanese supermarkets.
MSG (monosodium glutamate, VetSin, Zest, Aromat) A granulated seasoning that makes dishes more savoury in the same way that sugar makes dishes sweeter or salt makes dishes saltier.
Mung-bean starch/flour (green bean starch) Ground from dried mung beans; used to make thin translucent noodles and jelly noodles.

Nagaimo See Japanese taro
Nam pla See Fish sauce
Nan-byar-gyi khao swè Burmese broad, flat wheat noodles similar to tagliatelle; unavailable overseas.
Naruto See Japanese fishcake
Nashi See Asian pear
Natto See Japanese fermented soya beans
Ngan bya yay See Fish sauce
Ngapi See Shrimp paste
Nori Dark green seaweed sold dried in sheets or strips; also ground to a powder (*aonori*) to use as a garnish.
Nước chấm Vietnamese dipping sauce. The most common version made from just fish sauce, lime juice or vinegar and sugar is known as *nước mắm pha* (mixed fish sauce).
Nước mắm See Fish sauce

Okonomiyaki Japanese pancake; also the name of the thick Worcestershire-like sauce that accompanies the dish.
Onsen tamago See Japanese egg
Oyster sauce Thick, sweet and savoury cooking sauce made from oysters as the name suggests.

Pad Thai word for stir-fry.
Pak choi (bok choy) Green leafy vegetable, similar to chard.
Palm sugar Dark brown sugar sold in tubs, or in blocks that need to be shaved before use.
Pancit Filipino word for noodles.
Patis See Fish sauce
Perilla See Shiso
Pig intestines (chitterlings, fat ends) Sold fresh or frozen; must be cleaned thoroughly and blanched before use.
Pork rinds Pork skin that has been

fried until crisp and aerated so that it resembles Quavers; *kaep moo* in Thai, *wet khao kyaw* in Burmese. Popular in Asia and South America.
Preserved mustard greens Chinese pickled vegetable found dried or wet in packets. I prefer the wet version.
Preserved radish Chinese pickled vegetable found dried or wet in packets.

Rakhine Ethnic group formerly known as the Arakanese, based in the Rakhine state in Burma (aka Myanmar).
Ramen Soup-based noodle dish from Japan.
Ramen egg (*nitamago, ajitsuke egg, hanjuku egg*) Japanese soft-boiled egg that has been marinated in a soy sauce mixture.
Rice flour Ground from rice; used as a thickener and to make some noodles.
Rice paper wrappers Round or square sheets made from rice flour, used to make Vietnamese spring rolls and summer rolls; found dried or frozen.
Rice vinegar (rice wine vinegar) Mild white vinegar.
Rock sugar (yellow rock sugar) Chinese sugar sold in boxes of rock-like lumps; smash into smaller pieces in a pestle and mortar or with a rolling pin before using.

Sake Japanese rice wine.
Salmon roe Large red or orange salmon eggs sold fresh (*ikura*) in Japanese supermarkets and in jars in Western supermarkets.
Salt-pickled Japanese apricot (*umeboshi*) *Ume* fruit, a type of Japanese apricot often mistranslated as a plum, pickled in salt and purple shiso; salty and extremely sour. Eaten in small quantities with rice or on noodles.
Sambal Chilli-based sauces of various types popular in Indonesia, Malaysia, Singapore, the southern Philippines, South Africa and Sri Lanka, as well as in the Netherlands.
Sambal oelek Indonesian chilli paste.
Samphire Edible plant found growing along shores.
Sawtooth herb (culantro, *ngò gai*) Like very strong coriander; a common Vietnamese garnish.
Shan Ethnic group based in the Shan State in Burma (aka Myanmar).
Shan fermented soybean cake A Shan food found in Thailand and Burma made of dried, salt-fermented soya beans that

have been pressed into discs; *bè bohk* literally 'rotten beans' in Burmese, *tua nao* in Shan. Can be bought online at Mum's House.

Shichimi pepper (*shichimi togarashi*) Japanese spice mixture containing 7 ingredients (*shichimi* means 7), usually coarsely ground dried red chilli, ground *sanshō* (prickly ash), roasted orange peel, black and white sesame seeds, hemp seeds and ground ginger.

Shiitake mushroom Earthy-flavoured mushroom found dried or fresh; good for stocks and frying.

Shimeji mushroom (*buna-shimeji, beech mushroom*) Small mushrooms sold fresh in clumps; good for frying and in sauces.

Shiso (perilla, beefsteak plant, *tia to*) Purple or green herb with a peppery, zesty flavour like a cross between basil and mint. Sold fresh in Vietnamese and Japanese supermarkets; also dried and ground.

Shoyu See Japanese soy sauce

Shrimp paste Popular pungent Asian ingredient made from fermented ground shrimps (and/or fish) mixed with salt. Some versions are wet (such as Vietnamese *mắm ruốc*, *mắm tép* and *mắm tôm*, and Filipino *bagoong alamang*) while others are sun-dried and sold in rectangular blocks or tubs (such as Malay *belacan* and Indonesian *terasi*). Burmese *ngapi* and Thai *kapi* come in wet, dry and paste forms.

Sichuan pepper Dried spice with a mouth-tingling effect; an important component in five spice. Ground and whole peppercorns are sold in jars.

Sichuan preserved vegetables (*zha cai*) Type of pickled mustard plant stem originating from the Sichuan province in China; spicy, sour and very salty.

Siu yuk Chinese crispy pork belly.

Soy sauce Made from fermented soya beans; dark soy sauce is best used to add colour and sweetness in cooking; light soy sauce is best for dressings and dips and to add a salty note when cooking. My favourite brand of both light and dark is Pearl River Bridge.

Sriracha A Thai chilli sauce that many are obsessed with; sold in bottles.

Star anise Fragrant sweet-smelling spice sold dried as individual star-shaped fruits; an important component in five spice.

Straw mushroom (paddy straw mushroom) Picked while immature before their veils rupture, so they resemble light bulbs. Sold tinned in brine; added to soups, stews and stir-fries.

Sumac Lemony spice used dried and ground to a powder in Mediterranean and Middle Eastern cooking.

Sweet wheat sauce (*tianmianjiang*) Thick, dark brown paste made from a type of Chinese steamed bun known as *mantou*, wheat flour, sugar, salt and yellow soybean sauce.

Tahini Sesame paste.

Tamarind Sweet and sour pod-like fruit; usually sold dried in blocks that need to be rehydrated before use. Tamarind paste sold in jars is usually sweetened so adjust seasoning accordingly if you need to use it.

Tapioca flour Ground from the starch extracted from the cassava plant; used as a thickener and to make some noodles.

Tau pok See Beancurd puffs

Tianjin preserved vegetables (*dong cai*) Shredded Tianjin cabbage preserved in salt; slightly sour and very salty. Sold in small earthenware pots.

Tempura Japanese fritters with a light batter (recipe on page 52).

Tenkasu Tempura crumbs or drippings similar to scraps popular in Northern England (see recipe on page 13).

Terasi See Shrimp paste

Thai basil (*Thai sweet basil*) Pungent, fresh aniseed-like green herb with purple stems; called *bai horapha* in Thai and *húng quế* in Vietnamese. Used as garnish for Pho or Spicy Lemongrass Beef Noodles.

Tobiko See Flying fish roe

Tofu Soya bean curd; usually found fresh packed in water. Firm tofu is suitable for frying and in sauce; silken or soft tofu is suitable for soups. Extra-soft tofu (*sundubu*) is used in Korean stews (*jigae*).

Tonkatsu Japanese fried pork dish similar to schnitzel; also the name of the thick Worcestershire-like sauce that accompanies the dish.

Torch ginger buds (ginger flower, torch lily, *bunga kantan*) Dark pink flowerbuds considered an essential ingredient in Tamarind Fish Laksa; unavailable overseas.

Tua nao See Shan fermented soybean cake

Turmeric A pungent yellow root available fresh or dried and ground. Used to add colouring and a gentle curry flavour in cooking.

Umeboshi See Japanese salt-pickled apricot

Vietnamese balm (Vietnamese lemon mint, *kinh giới*) Bright green herb with serrated edges; tastes like lemon and mint (hence its alternate English name).

Vietnamese coriander (Vietnamese mint, laksa leaf, hot mint, *rau răm, daun kesom*) A blade-like herb used in Vietnamese dishes and for laksa; similar in flavour to coriander.

Wasabi Pungent, fiery Japanese root similar to horseradish; sold fresh in Japanese supermarkets and as a paste in tubes in Western supermarkets.

Water spinach (water morning glory, *rau muống, kankong*) Leafy, hollow-stemmed vegetable similar in flavour to watercress.

Winter melon (ash gourd, wax gourd) Vine fruit that can be picked young, peeled and eaten as a sweet fruit, or picked when mature and eaten as a vegetable. When mature, it has waxy skin and white flesh that turns translucent when cooked. Cucumber can be used as a substitute.

Wok hei The flavour, texture and 'essence' imparted by a hot wok during stir-frying. The food must be cooked in a seasoned wok over an open flame while being stirred and tossed quickly.

Wonton wrappers Pastry sheets used to make wontons (Chinese dumplings); sold fresh or frozen.

Wood-ear mushroom (Chinese black fungus, tree ear, Jew's ear, jelly ear) A fungus sold dried in packets; rehydrate before using. Called *kikurage* in Japanese.

Yakisoba Japanese fried noodle dish; also the name of the thick Worcestershire-like sauce that accompanies the dish.

Yellow soybean sauce (salted soybeans, yellow bean sauce, yellow soybean paste) Fermented yellow (actually light brown) soya beans in a sauce or paste. Yeo's is my favourite brand.

Yuzu Japanese citrus sold as bottled juice or as dried peel.

STOCKISTS

Most Asian ingredients can be bought from larger branches of Waitrose, Tesco, Sainsburys, Morrisons and Asda. If you're based in London and its suburbs, my favourite shops are as follows:

Chinese ingredients
See Woo, New Loon Moon or Loong Fung in Chinatown (and their suburban branches).

Korean ingredients
Centrepoint Food Store on St Giles High St near Tottenham Court Road, and countless shops in New Malden (aka Koreatown).

Japanese ingredients
Japan Centre on Shaftesbury Avenue or Arigato on Brewer Street.

Vietnamese ingredients
Longdan on Hackney Road and in Elephant & Castle.

Malaysian and Filipino ingredients
Chuang Lee off Bugsby's Way in Charlton.

If you can't get to any of these in person, the following shops also deliver online orders:

Chinese ingredients
Wai Yee Hong
www.waiyeehong.com
Eastgate Oriental City
Eastgate Road
Eastville
Bristol BS5 6XX

Thai ingredients
Tawana
www.tawana.co.uk
16–20 Chepstow Road
London W2 5BD
and
243-245 Plaistow Road
London E15 3EU

Japanese ingredients
Japan Centre
www.japancentre.com
19 Shaftesbury Ave
London W1D 7ED

Burmese ingredients
Mum's House
www.mumhouse.com
78 Mannock Road
Wood Green
London N22 6AA

Other specialist ingredients
Anything else you can dream of can usually be found on this website:
Sous Chef
www.souschef.co.uk

INDEX